BATTLES & LEADERS SERIES

OUTWITTING FORREST

THE TUPELO CAMPAIGN IN MISSISSIPPI,

JUNE 22–JULY 23, 1864

Edwin C. Bearss
edited by David A. Powell

SB

Savas Beatie
California

Savas Beatie Battles & Leaders Series

First edition, first printing

ISBN-13 (hardcover): 978-1-61121-670-7
ISBN-13 (ebook): 978-1-954547-60-5

Library of Congress Cataloging-in-Publication Data

Names: Bearss, Edwin C., author. | Powell, David A. (David Alan), 1961- editor.
Title: Outwitting Forrest : the Tupelo Campaign in Mississippi, June 22-July 23, 1864 / by Edwin C Bearss ; edited by David A. Powell.
Other titles: Tupelo Campaign in Mississippi, June 22-July 23, 1864.
Description: El Dorado Hills, CA : Savas Beatie LLC, [2023] | Series: Savas Beatie Battles & Leaders Series | Includes bibliographical references and index. | Summary: "Few students of the Civil War know that legendary historian Edwin C. Bearss produced a classic study on the little-known but significant Tupelo Campaign. It is published here for the first time, with the assistance of award-winning author David A. Powell. The result is an exceptional study that has finally been made available to the general reading public as part of the Savas Beatie Battles & Leaders Series"-- Provided by publisher.
Identifiers: LCCN 2022056769 | ISBN 9781611216707 (hardcover) | ISBN 9781954547605 (ebook)
Subjects: LCSH: Tupelo, Battle of, Tupelo, Miss., 1864.
Classification: LCC E476.84 .B43 2023 | DDC 973.7/37--dc23/eng/20230113
LC record available at https://lccn.loc.gov/2022056769

Savas Beatie
989 Governor Drive, Suite 102
El Dorado Hills, CA 95762
916-941-6896 / sales@savasbeatie.com / www.savasbeatie.com

Dedication

To the memory of Edwin C. Bearss.

To my wife, Anne.

Other Titles in the

Battles & Leaders Series

Thirteen Months in Dixie, or, the Adventures of a Federal Prisoner in Texas: Including the Red River Campaign, Imprisonment at Camp Ford, and Escape Overland to Liberated, Shreveport, 1864–1865,
by W. F. Oscar Federhen,
edited by Jeannine Surette Honstein and Steven A. Knowlton

The Battle of Jackson, Mississippi, May 14, 1863,
by Chris Mackowski

The Johnson-Gilmor Cavalry Raid Around Baltimore, July 10–13, 1864,
by Eric J. Wittenberg

Table of Contents

List of Maps

Foreword

by David A. Powell

THE AUTHOR of this study, National Park Historian Emeritus Edwin C. Bearss, is rightfully a legend in Civil War circles. Though he died in 2020, Ed's decades of scholarship, activism, and presence in public history made him the face of preservation and interpretation. His work at many Civil War battlefield parks, especially his detailed mapping of many engagements, has underpinned the work of dozens of other authors. His distinctive speaking style and entertaining manner can best be remembered through his work on the successful Ken Burns documentary "The Civil War."

Unfortunately, I only met Ed Bearss twice, both times during speaking engagements for the Chicago Civil War Round Table. Of course, I have heard countless secondhand tales of the man. Perhaps my favorite was related to me by Chickamauga Park Historian James Ogden. According to Jim, he was holding up a map at a stop on one of the many tours he routinely conducted, so Ed could use it illustrate a point. The two were perched on the edge of a bluff, where Ed was striking the map so vigorously with his swagger stick that Ogden staggered for a second or two and nearly fell down the slope. Fortunately, he regained his balance before taking the tumble. Ed, whose enthusiasm remained undaunted, barely noticed.

Ed Bearss served in the Marine Corps during World War Two and was badly wounded in the Pacific Theater. After two years of recovery, he returned stateside to pursue a history career and entered the National Park Service. He earned multiple honors and accolades and penned numerous books and articles. Many of those writings were ahead of their time in terms of clarity, comprehension, and analysis. Certainly, his study of Tupelo falls into that category.

Nathan Bedford Forrest is one of the most romanticized, vilified, and ultimately mythologized figures of the war. The cult of personality surrounding him has produced generations of outsized legends. Separating fact from fiction can be difficult. I found this to be true while working on Forrest during the Chickamauga Campaign, as documented in my own work *Failure in the Saddle: Nathan Bedford Forrest, Joseph Wheeler, and the Confederate Cavalry in the Chickamauga Campaign* (Savas Beatie, 2010). Sifting truth from legend is equally difficult regarding Forrest's 1864 activities in Mississippi, which included, among other actions, Brice's Crossroads (June 10) and Tupelo (July 14-15). The two battles are an interesting study in contrasts. The former was one of the more complete Confederate victories of the war, while the latter was a sharp—and bloody—defeat. Forrest was in overall command at Brice's Crossroads, but that was not the case at Tupelo, where Lt. Gen. Stephen D. Lee was in overall command, which has sometimes been used to overlook Forrest's own mistakes there.

By 1864, the war in Mississippi had become something of a sideshow. The major players, including Gens. U. S. Grant, William T. Sherman, and Joseph E. Johnston, had departed the theater for campaigns in Virginia and Georgia, and both sides stripped the state of troops to support those efforts. As a result, the engagements in Mississippi that summer were waged on a much smaller scale than those that had come before. They were not, however, unimportant—especially since one of General Sherman's major concerns was that Forrest might slip away from the state to fall on Sherman's supply lines and disrupt the railroads in Tennessee. The fact that Forrest never managed to do so is directly attributable to Federal actions in Mississippi, most notably those conducted by Brig. Gen. Samuel Sturgis at Brice's Crossroads and Maj. Gen. A. J. Smith at Tupelo. Significantly, Smith's July victory at Tupelo helped ensure that Forrest would not go elsewhere.

At just one acre, the Tupelo National Battlefield site has the distinction of being one of the smallest NPS-administered Civil War battlefields in the country. Almost nothing had been written about the battle when Ed was tasked in 1969 with writing a study of the site with a view toward improving its interpretation. He produced not just a site assessment, but a 223-page monograph of the campaign and battle. It was the first modern study of the affair, supported by his usual careful map work. Though it was subsequently published by the Department of the Interior and sold through U.S. Government bookstores, Bearss's *The Tupelo Campaign* remains a rarity in both institutional and private collections.

In an effort to redress that obscurity, publisher Theodore P. (Ted) Savas decided that *Tupelo* needed a new edition. Savas Beatie has a history of rescuing "lost" manuscripts and long-out-of-date classics. O. Edward Cunningham's marvelous thesis, published as *Shiloh and the Western Campaign of 1862* in 2009, is a prime example of the former. Editors Timothy B. Smith and Gary D. Joiner prepared the final manuscript, which among other things, included appending the text with notes where more modern scholarship diverged from or complimented Cunningham's insights. Ted asked me to tackle *Tupelo*, and after a little convincing I readily agreed. We decided to use the same technique—modern notes separated from original notes by a || symbol, which indicate where Bearss's original citation ends and my own comments begin.[1]

I found *Tupelo* to be an excellent operational and tactical study worthy of republication, especially since more recent scholarship on the campaign is limited and consists primarily of Thomas Parson's excellent study *Work for Giants: The Campaign and Battle of Tupelo/Harrisburg, Mississippi, June-July, 1864* (Kent State, 2014). It is worth noting that Parson cited Bearss regularly and often found his conclusions remarkably on point. I did not add a great deal of editorial content because there was not much by way of dissenting scholarship and little new of discovery since Bearss's original publication now more than half a century old.

My hope is that readers will enjoy this new addition, which is part of the new and very attractive Savas Beatie Battles & Leaders Series. The classic look and original design, coupled with the opportunity to introduce *Tupelo* to a new generation of readers, would I believe have made Ed very happy.

Acknowledgments

First and foremost, I must thank Ed Bearss, who produced this study in 1969 while working for the National Park Service. Ed was the first historian in decades to take an interest in the events of the Tupelo Campaign, and it stands the test of time, yet more decades later. It was an honor to edit this project for a modern audience.

Thanks are also due to Theodore P. Savas, who reached out to me when he decided he wanted to republish it for a modern audience. I jumped at the chance. Along with Ted, I must also thank the crack sales and production team that is

1 An example of the rebirth of an out-of-print classic is one penned by Ed himself, his magnificent trilogy *The Campaign for Vicksburg* (Savas Beatie, 2021).

Savas Beatie, who have now worked with me on numerous projects and made each and every book better. I hope we can work together on many more projects to come.

Finally, I want to thank my wife Anne, who always supports my writing endeavors.

David A. Powell
March 2023

Foreword

by Edwin C. Bearss

THIS REPORT has been prepared to satisfy the research needs as enumerated in "RSP, NATR-H-15, Battle of Tupelo (Tupelo National Battlefield Site), Section 3-D, Natchez Trace Parkway, Lee County, Mississippi." To accomplish this, the campaign culminating in the battle of Tupelo on July 14, 1864, has been studied and analyzed, and a documented narrative and troop movement maps prepared. Recommendations have been made as to the transfer and up-grading of interpretive facilities.

Several persons have assisted in the preparation of this report. Thanks are due Claude Gentry of Baldwyn, Mississippi, for sharing his knowledge of the area; Frank Sarles for proofreading the final draft; and Miss Kathy See for the diligent manner in which she typed the manuscript.

E. C. B.

1

Sherman Sends A. J. Smith to Destroy Forrest

THE RANKING Union officers in Memphis were stunned to be awakened on June 12, 1864, to learn that Brig. Gen. Samuel D. Sturgis had been routed by Confederate forces led by Maj. Gen. Nathan Bedford Forrest at Brices Crossroads two days before. Sturgis himself was at Collierville, Tennessee, 21 miles away, with his shattered command. It was from there that he had sent a message that did anything but reassure his immediate superior, Maj. Gen. Cadwallader C. Washburn, the officer responsible for holding West Tennessee for the Union. He had telegraphed, "Trains have just arrived. Do you wish me to hold this place or withdraw when I get my debris away?"[1]

1 *The War of the Rebellion; A Compilation of the Official Records of the Union and Confederate Armies* (70 vols., in 128 parts, Washington, 1880-1900). Series I. Vol. 39, pt. 2, 107 (Hereinafter cited as *O.R.*) General Washburn commanded the District of West Tennessee, with headquarters at Memphis. | | Cadwallader C. Washburn was brother to U.S. Congressman Elihu C. Washburne of Galena, Illinois, who was in turn General Grant's political patron in Washington. The Washburns of Maine were a wealthy, well-connected clan. Cadwallader followed his brother Elihu west, settling in Wisconsin, where he practiced law and served in Congress for three terms, 1855-1861. Cadwallader raised the 2nd Wisconsin Cavalry over the winter of 1861-1862, which was accepted into federal service in March. He was promoted to brigadier general four months later, on July 16, 1862, and to major general the next year. He commanded a cavalry division during the Vicksburg Campaign, and then spent his war

Before doing anything else, Washburn had to make certain that the Rebels, who were said to be pressing Sturgis's people, did not make a dash into Memphis. An aide left Washburn's headquarters at 1 a.m. with a message apprising the veteran corps commander Brig. Gen. Andrew J. Smith of the disaster, and directing him to have 2,000 infantry at the depot of the Memphis and Charleston Railroad as soon as possible. The soldiers, when they fell out, were to have three days' rations in their haversacks and 100 rounds of ammunition on their person. To insure that Smith moved promptly, he was made to understand that "the case is urgent."[2]

A hardbitten "old army" man, A. J. Smith, had just reached Memphis with 6,000 men of the detachments of the XVI and XVII Corps that had participated in the ill-starred Red River Campaign.

Smith, whose command was en route to rejoin Maj. Gen. William T. Sherman's Army Group in northwest Georgia, had been halted at Memphis. Orders had been received on June 6 from Sherman, dated two days before, for Smith to organize a force of from 6,000 to 10,000 men to cooperate in an attack on Mobile by way of Pascagoula.[3]

---

mainly in occupation duties. E. B. Quiner, *The Military History of Wisconsin: A Record of the Civil and Military Patriotism of the State, in the War for the Union, with a History of the Campaigns in which Wisconsin Soldiers have been Conspicuous—Regimental Histories—Sketches of Distinguished Officers—The Roll of the Illustrious Dead—Movements of the Legislature and State Officers, etc.* (Chicago: 1866), 900.

2 Ibid., 109.

3 Ibid., 79. || Maj. Gen. Andrew Jackson Smith, born in Bucks County, Pennsylvania, was 49 years old in the summer of 1864. He graduated from the Military Academy at West Point in 1838; classmates included Union Maj. Gen. Irvin McDowell as well as Confederate generals P. G. T. Beauregard, William J. Hardee, Edward Johnston, and Carter L. Stevenson. Commissioned into the 1st Dragoons, Smith spent the next two decades in mounted service across the western frontier, fighting Indians and seeing action in the Mexican War. He served with the Army of the Tennessee under Grant up through

Smith could move with alacrity. He contacted the leader of the Third Division, XVI Corps, Col. David Moore, and told him to turn out his 3d Brigade. As the 49th Illinois had re-enlisted and was about to leave for home on veteran furlough, Moore was directed to substitute another regiment to insure that when the brigade boarded the waiting cars it would muster 2,000 effectives. Moore was a capable subordinate. Besides issuing the necessary orders to his 3d Brigade commander, he alerted Col. James I. Gilbert of his 2d Brigade to hold his men ready to take the field at a moment's notice.[4]

Moore's bluecoats were at Collierville before sufficient details concerning Sturgis's defeat had reached Washburn to enable him to contact his superiors. Secretary of War Edwin M. Stanton was informed that Sturgis with 3,000 cavalry, 5,000 infantry, and 16 pieces of artillery had been "completely worsted, losing most of the artillery and infantry." Latest information from the front was that Sturgis was at Collierville, with Forrest in pursuit. The presence of A. J. Smith's command enabled Washburn to assure the Secretary that Memphis could be held.[5]

A message was also forwarded to General Sherman. Sherman, whose "Army Group" was engaged in a campaign aimed at the destruction of the Confederate Army of Tennessee and who was responsible for the dispatch of Sturgis's column, was told of the defeat. Sturgis, Washburn

---

Vicksburg. After that citadel's surrender in July 1863, Smith was detached to various other theaters, most notably to support Nathaniel P. Banks in the Red River Campaign. One soldier described Smith as "of small stature, with rather brusque, abrupt manners, sometimes verging in irascibility, yet was popular with his troops, and shunned none of the hardships to which they were subjected." Leslie J. Perry, "Andrew Jackson Smith," *Twenty Seventh Annual Reunion of the Association of Graduates of the United States Military Academy at West Point* (Saginaw, MI: Seaman & Peters, 1896).

4 Ibid., 109.

5 Ibid., 106.

telegraphed, had been "badly cut up." Although he had but few details, "it was a very bad affair." Sherman was notified of A. J. Smith's arrival with 6,000 foot soldiers but little artillery. Word had arrived from Maj. Gen. Edward R. S. Canby that the Trans-Mississippi Confederates were concentrating against Maj. Gen. Frederick Steele in Arkansas. This information, coupled with Sturgis's rout, made Washburn question the wisdom of the orders releasing A. J. Smith to Canby for a thrust on Mobile.[6]

It took two days for Washburn's telegram to find Sherman at his Big Shanty, Georgia, headquarters. He was understandably depressed by the news, for if Forrest were not destroyed he would be free to fall upon and wreck the Nashville & Chattanooga Railroad over which Sherman received the tools of war and the rations to subsist his huge "Army Group." Under these circumstances, the Mobile expedition would have to be junked. If General Canby could "spare Smith's command, it should go out and meet Forrest." As Confederate Lt. Gen. Leonidas Polk and all his corps of infantry, as well as Brig. Gen. William H. Jackson's cavalry, was in Georgia, Sherman could not "see what Forrest can have except his cavalry" and militia. But whatever Forrest's force, it "should be met and defeated at any and all cost," he wired Washburn.[7]

6 Ibid. Canby had written Washburn from Natchez, on June 8, that information had reached him that Confederate General Edmund Kirby Smith was said to be concentrating his troops "for the purpose of operating against General Steele." As the line of the Arkansas "must be held," Washburn would hold himself ready to reinforce Steele. Ibid., 89.

7 Ibid., 115. General Polk with two infantry divisions (French's and Loring's) and Jackson's cavalry division had reinforced Gen. Joseph E. Johnston's Army of Tennessee in northwest Georgia. Polk on May 9 had turned over responsibility for the Department of Alabama, Mississippi, and East Louisiana to Maj. Gen. Stephen D. Lee. Ibid., 590. || Of the approximately 40,000 Rebel troops assigned to defend the department in April 1864, Polk took 16,000 of them to Georgia. Another 1,000 were en route to Virginia. After further subtracting the forces assigned to defend Mobile, the gulf coast, and northern Alabama,

Meanwhile, General Sturgis had reached Memphis, where on the 13th he discussed his defeat with Washburn and Smith. What Washburn heard enabled him to scale down Union losses, which first reports placed at between 2,000 and 4,000 to 1,500 to 2,000 men, 14 pieces of artillery, and 130 wagons. Sturgis and his officers placed Forrest's strength at from 15,000 to 20,000. With their interior rail lines, the Confederates within 24 hours could shift this force to Mobile. If Sherman were agreeable, Washburn with Smith's and the other Memphis troops would make "a demonstration thirty or forty miles out, which will tend to keep the force that whipped Sturgis away from" Sherman.[8]

To be prepared for this eventuality, Washburn on June 14 alerted A. J. Smith to hold his corps "in readiness to march on the morning on the 16th." He was to have 3,000 foot soldiers at the yards by 6 a.m., and the remainder

---

there were only about 12,000 Rebels left in Mississippi. Forrest's command reported 9,829 officers and men present for duty at the end of April. Steven H. Newton, *Lost for the Cause, The Confederate Army in 1864* (Mason City, IA: 2000), 279-295.

8 Ibid., 118. | | Samuel D. Sturgis was a Military Academy graduate, class of 1846. He saw service in the Mexican War and on the Western frontier; in 1861 he was stationed at Fort Smith, Arkansas. He served under Nathaniel Lyon at the battle of Wilson's Creek, inheriting command of Lyon's army after that officer's death in combat. Transferred east, he served in Virginia in the IX Corps. During the Second Bull Run Campaign, he was trying to organize rail transport for his brigade when he was informed that the movement had been prohibited by Federal army commander John Pope. In response, the possibly inebriated Sturgis informed the train conductor that "I don't care for John Pope one pinch of owl dung," a line oft quoted in histories of the war. He subsequently served in Kentucky and other western states until his ignominious defeat at Brice's Crossroads. After the war he had an active career out west, including a part in the Nez Pearce Campaign of 1877. He 1881, after a contentious congressional process during which many of the men who served under him at Brice's Crossroads vehemently opposed his nomination, Sturgis became governor of the Soldier's Home in Washington DC. He resigned from that position in 1886 and died three years later. Ezra J. Warner, *Generals in Blue, Lives of the Union Commanders* (Baton Rouge, LA: 1964), 486-487.

BRIG. GEN. SAMUEL D. STURGIS

Sturgis was badly defeated at the battle of Brice's Crossroads.

Library of Congress

there by 2 p.m. The men were to take three days' rations in their haversacks and 40 rounds of ammunition in their cartridge boxes. Smith's artillery was to take the field at the same time with full units of fire in caissons and limbers.[9]

9 Ibid., 119.

The leader of Washburn's mounted arm, the hell-for-leather cavalryman Brig. Gen. Benjamin H. Grierson, was alerted to be prepared for the movement. Grierson, who had his command post at White's Station, called for his horse soldiers to keep a sharp watch to prevent Rebel raiders from tearing up the railroad. Patrols were en route to take possession of Lafayette and Germantown.[10]

The officer in charge of the railroad shook his head when he learned of Washburn's plans. It would be impossible for his locomotives and cars to make the trip to Moscow and return to Memphis by 2 p.m. In addition, he did not have sufficient cars to handle more than 2,000 men on a trip. When Washburn learned of this, he altered Smith's instructions. Two thousand troops would be at the Memphis & Charleston depot at the stipulated hour on the 16th, and the remainder at 6 a.m. on the 17th. Besides their rations and ammunition, the soldiers were to take with them blankets, shelter-tents, and cooking utensils.[11]

There was a change in plans, however, and Washburn determined to send the 1st Brigade, U.S. Colored Troops commanded by Col. Edward Bouton to guard the working parties repairing the Memphis & Charleston Railroad, east of Collierville. The Negro regiments marched on June 18 and took position between Collierville and Lafayette. A. J. Smith and his division and brigade commanders would be able to take advantage of the extra days in Memphis to perfect the outfitting of their units for the anticipated hard campaign.

Forty-eight hours had passed, and Sherman, a volatile individual, had become increasingly disturbed by the events in northeastern Mississippi and their possible repercussions on his Georgia campaigns. Especially irritating was an article carried in the Atlanta papers of the 13th, reporting that

10 Ibid.

11 Ibid., 122. Gilbert's brigade was selected to move on the 16th. Ibid.

BRIG. GEN. ANDREW JACKSON SMITH

Smith was tasked by William T. Sherman to "pursue and kill" Rebel cavalryman Nathan Bedford Forrest.

Library of Congress

at Brices Crossroads, Forrest had had only two brigades. Sturgis therefore had deliberately misled his superiors about the Confederates' strength. Telegraphing Washburn on June 16, he exploded, "It is all nonsense about Sturgis being attacked by 15,000 or 20,000. He was whipped by a force inferior to his own. Let the matter be critically investigated."[12]

12 Ibid., 124.

At the same time, Sherman issued orders for the organization at Memphis of

> as large a force as possible..., with Generals A. J. Smith or [Joseph A.] Mower in command, to pursue Forrest on foot, devastating the land over which he has passed or may pass, and make him and the people of Tennessee and Mississippi realize that, although a bold, daring, and successful leader, he will bring ruin and misery on any country where he may pause or tarry. If we do not punish Forrest and the people now, the whole effect of our past conquests will be lost.[13]

General Sherman's message of June 14, regarding the suspension of the Mobile Expedition and the dispatch of A. J. Smith to deal with Forrest's Rebel cavalry, was 48 hours in reaching Memphis. On its receipt, Washburn replied that he had anticipated his superior—orders had already been issued for Smith to go out and hold or whip Forrest.[14] He had also notified General Canby in New Orleans that he was sending a column against Forrest. Supplies would be a problem, as the raids and counter-raids had made a desert of the country between Memphis and the Mobile & Ohio Railroad. The Memphis & Charleston Railroad was in operation to Collierville, and fatigue parties had been turned to, and it was hoped to have the cars running as far as Grand Junction by June 20 or 21.[15]

Washburn's message of the 14th arrived at Big Shanty on the 18th. Sherman was delighted to learn of the march of A. J. Smith's column. As an inducement to Smith's ranking subordinate, Sherman telegraphed, "Say to General Mower that I want him advanced, and if he will whip Forrest I will

13 Ibid., 123.

14 Ibid., 124.

15 Ibid., 125. Collierville was 21 miles east of Memphis.

pledge him my influence for a major-general, and will ask the President as a personal favor to hold a vacancy for him."[16]

To make good on his promise, Sherman telegraphed President Abraham Lincoln that A. J. Smith and Mower had been ordered to "pursue and kill Forrest." As Mower, in his opinion, was "one of the gamest men in our service," Sherman desired this favor, "should accident befell me."[17]

The Memphis & Charleston Railroad, by June 21, had been repaired as far as Grissom's Bridge. On receipt of this information, General Mower alerted the men of his command, the First Division, XVI Corps, to be at the depot ready to entrain at 7 a.m. on the 22d. The camps would be left as they were with a guard of convalescents.[18] General Grierson was charged with providing an escort for the division's train and artillery, and orders were issued for the 2d Iowa Cavalry to be at General Smith's Poplar Street headquarters at 9

16 Ibid., 130.

17 Ibid., 142. | | Joseph A. Mower was a pre-war professional officer, directly commissioned into the 1st U.S. Infantry in 1855, after having served an earlier stint in the U.S. Engineers during the Mexican War. Sherman and Smith regarded Mower as one of the most aggressive and effective officers in the U.S. Service. He was popular with the troops, as well: "The *New York Times* claimed he was brave to a fault, 'absolutely without any sense of danger, he seemed to relish above everything else the tumult of battle.' Cloyd Byner, the historian of the 47th Illinois Infantry agreed, saying that there was 'no lover more impatient for his mistress than Mower for war's troubles.' He had a dangerous tendency of riding far forward to observe the fighting, 'an almost uncontrollable impulse to mingle with the skirmish line.' Not only was he a hard fighter, he was an equally hard drinker, often combining the two activities. On the morning of October 4, 1862, at the Battle of Corinth, he was drunk when he led a patrol that skirmished with the enemy and ended up with a nasty neck wound and a few hours as a prisoner. A month later he was a brigadier general. Capt. Theodore Carter of the 7th Minnesota made a canny observation of his division commander when he said, 'Gen. Mower was a good military man, when he was sober. But he could not stand success. If he accomplished his designs one day, the next he was quite sure to be full.'" Thomas E. Parson, *Work for Giants, The Campaign and Battle of Tupelo/Harrisburg, Mississippi, June-July 1864* (Kent, OH: 2014), 139.

18 Ibid., 139.

a.m. on the 23d. The cavalry was to send its ammunition forward by rail and use its wagons for forage.[19]

On the 22d the cars were used to shuttle the infantry units of Mower's division from Memphis to Grissom's Bridge, where they camped for the night. As the trains rumbled eastward, the troops exchanged good natured cheers and jeers with the men of Colonel Bouton's brigade (the 61st and 68th U.S. Colored Troops, and Battery I, 2d U. S. Colored Artillery) guarding the railroad on either side of Lafayette. Mower's brigades were formed the next morning and marched to Moscow.[20]

Colonel Moore on the 22d was alerted that the railroad would be clear the next day for the movement of his division. Col. Edward H. Wolfe's brigade was to go first and would be at the station at 6:30 a.m. The division trains were to start for the front at 8:30 on the 24th, via the State Line road.

Wolfe's people boarded the cars as scheduled. Near Lafayette the train was fired into by Confederate partisans posted in underbrush along the right-of-way. Several men were killed or wounded, while others in the excitement leaped off the cars. The engineer pushed down the throttle; the locomotive picked up speed, and was soon out of range. Several of the men who jumped from the cars were captured and murdered by the partisans. The train reached Moscow without further adventure, and Wolfe's troops scrambled off the flat cars and went into camp alongside Mower's people. Moore's other two brigades (Murray's and Gilbert's) were transferred from Memphis to Moscow on the 24th and 25th without incident.[21]

The regimental historian of the 32d Iowa of Gilbert's brigade reported that at the time the regiment entrained,

19 Ibid., 139-140.

20 *O.R.*, Series I., Vol. 39, pt. 1, 259, 300. Bouton's troops had been in position along the railroad since June 18.

21 Ibid., 295; O.R., Series I, Vol. 39, pt. 2, 141.

many of the soldiers were "suffering from dysentery and malarial diseases, the effects of the Red river campaign." Before taking the field, the regiment had received a detail of recruits and a number of men had been returned from the hospital, so it mustered 416 effectives on the morning of June 24.[22]

General A. J. Smith, who had transferred his headquarters to Moscow to be with his troops, notified General Washburn on the 24th that he had checked with the pioneers and the bridge across the Wolf River would be rebuilt by Sunday night, the 26th. As soon as the bridge was declared open for rail traffic, Smith would push on to La Grange. A detachment of cavalry had visited that village on the 23d and found it clear of Confederates. Once his corps had reached La Grange, the railroad would be employed to build-up stockpiles of rations, forage, and ammunition. According to his scouts and spies, Forrest was at Tupelo on the Mobile & Ohio Railroad.[23]

General Grierson had kept the 3,200 horse soldiers of his division busy guarding the railroad, escorting wagon trains, and patrolling. Col. Edward F. Winslow's brigade, serving as escort to the army's trains, left Memphis at 9 a.m. on the 24th, and spent the night at the Ponds near Collierville. The next day, the column pushed on to Moscow, and went into bivouac on Wolf River.[24] Grierson's other brigade commander, Col. Datus B. Coon, employed several of his regiments to escort trains, and one, the 7th Kansas, to scout and protect the fatigue parties repairing the railroad.[25]

On June 25 General Smith had Grierson send a cavalry patrol eastward along the right-of-way to ascertain the

22 John Scott, *Story of the 32d Iowa Infantry Volunteers* (Nevada, Iowa, 1896), 290.

23 *O.R.*, Series I, Vol. 39, pt. 2, 143.

24 *O.R.*, Series I, Vol. 39, pt. 1, 304, 305.

25 Ibid., 315-316, 318-319; *O.R.*, Series I, Vol. 39, pt. 2, 141, 142.

condition of the tracks between Moscow and Saulsbury. The troopers returned the next day and reported not much work would be required to enable the trains to run to the latter point. Grierson was accordingly told to move all the cavalry that had reached Moscow and had been paid forward to La Grange.[26] Upon checking with his brigade commanders, Grierson discovered that all the regiments had been paid, except the 3d Iowa Cavalry. When the division, spearheaded by the 9th Illinois Cavalry, rode out on the morning of June 27, the 3d Iowa stayed in camp and draw their pay and rations.[27]

General Smith was delighted on the evening of the 26th to see that the bridge across the Wolf River had been finished. Hereafter all trains leaving Memphis would be able to make the run to La Grange. Before he pushed on, Smith asked Washburn, "Am I to take the colored regiments (Bouton's) now at La Payette as part of my command?" If so, they would be invaluable as a wagon guard. If not, some of them should be advanced to Moscow to protect the bridge over Wolf River.[28]

Washburn, recognizing the merit in Smith's suggestion, ordered Bouton to report to Smith. He also increased Bouton's force by one-third, as the train which chugged eastward to Moscow on the 27th carried the 57th U.S. Colored Troops.[29]

26 *O.R.*, Series I, Vol. 39, pt. 2, 147.

27 *O.R.*, Series I, Vol. 39, pt. 1, 305, 307, 316.

28 *O.R.*, Series I, Vol. 39, pt. 2, 147.

29 *O.R.*, Series I, Vol. 39, pt. 1, 300. || Colonel Edward Bouton was a Chicago businessman (originally from New York) who raised Battery I, 1st Illinois light artillery for war service in 1862. He and his gunners played a dramatic role in defending Grant's final line on the first day at Shiloh, April 6, 1862. Subsequently Bouton transferred to the infantry to command the newly forming 59th United States Colored Troops, and then, a brigade. He and his men fought well at Brices Crossroads despite the larger disaster to Union arms, covering the retreat of what had become a panicked mob of blue-coated

Smith's infantry on June 27 broke camp, crossed Wolf River, and made the 11-mile march to La Grange. The day was frightfully hot and humid, and large numbers of men straggled. When the 32d Iowa stopped and camped at 2 p.m., only 20 men answered when roll was called. General Mower, who brought up the rear, found a large number of bluecoats "lying by the roadside, overcome with heat." He stopped, dismounted, and "kindly urged them . . . to move on, as they were in the rear and liable to be taken prisoner by roving bands of the enemy." By midnight most of the stragglers had rejoined their units, which had bivouacked in the Wolf River bottom.[30]

Orders were issued by Smith for Grierson to have his horse soldiers advance to Saulsbury on the 28th. Now that Bouton's regiments would be joining him, Smith asked Washburn to see that cavalry from Memphis was detailed to picket all roads between Germantown and La Grange. Smith would remain at La Grange until his magazines had been stockpiled, which would not be earlier than Thursday, the 30th. Time would not be wasted, as the repair crews had been detailed to put the railroad between La Grange and Pocahontas in running order. Smith planned to move slowly and deliberately and be ready "to meet Forrest if he comes within one week."[31]

Winslow's cavalry brigade on June 28 rode forward from La Grange and camped in and around Saulsbury. Here it was rejoined by the 3d Iowa. Grierson's other brigade. Coon's, remained at La Grange.[32] Meanwhile, Bouton's

---

infantry and cavalrymen. Kenneth Bancroft Moore, "Fort Pillow, Forrest, and the United States Colored Troops in 1864," *Tennessee Historical Quarterly*, vol. 54, no. 2 (Summer, 1995), 112-123.

30 Scott, *Story of the 32d Iowa*, 290-91. Two trains also reached La Grange during the day-one carrying supplies and the other the construction battalion.

31 *O.R.*, Series I, Vol. 39, pt. 1, 279; *O.R.*, Series I, Vol. 39, pt. 2, 149-150.

32 *O.R.*, Series I, Vol. 39, pt. 1, 305, 307, 315.

brigade, part moving by rail and the remainder marching, had reached La Grange. There Bouton reported to Smith that the effective strength of his unit was 1,899.[33] By dusk on the 28th, Smith had concentrated all his infantry, except one regiment guarding the bridge at Grissom's Creek, in and around La Grange. As that unit would be called up in the morning, Smith requested that Washburn have the regiment currently posted at Lafayette provide a company to protect the structure from bridge-burners.[34]

Washburn on June 27 cautioned Smith that "you had better be in no hurry in leaving the line of railroad with your infantry and artillery, but seem to be engaged in repairing the road and moving on to Corinth." He believed that as long as they held Forrest in Mississippi, they were "doing good work," but if they could decoy him up to Corinth it would be "a great deal better than to go down to Tupelo after him." If, however, Forrest failed to fall for the ruse, Smith would have to go after him. Reports reaching Memphis indicated that Forrest had a brigade at Corinth, and Washburn suggested that a strong cavalry column be sent to strike the Mobile & Ohio, six miles south of Corinth, to see what it could develop.[35]

While Smith agreed with Washburn, he did not believe Forrest would venture an attack on the Federals until they had placed several days' marches between their column and the Memphis and Charleston. Not wishing to exhaust his cavalry before his infantry was ready to leave La Grange, Smith vetoed the proposed dash on the Mobile & Ohio. About this time, Smith received bad news from his chief of ordnance—"a large portion" of his ammunition

33 Ibid., 300; Robert Cowden, *A Brief Sketch of the Organization and Service of the Fifty-Ninth Regiment of United States Colored Infantry* (Dayton, 1883), 126-127.

34 *O.R.*, Series I, Vol. 39, pt. 2, 150.

35 Ibid., 149.

was worthless. The condemned ammunition would be returned to Memphis by special train. Smith was happy, however, that this discovery had been made while it was still possible to restock the La Grange magazines.[36] Several days passed before the ammunition was replaced, and on July 2 Washburn was able to notify Smith that he was to leave the railroad as soon as he was ready.[37]

Brig. Gen. Edward Hatch of the cavalry returned to duty, on the expiration of his sick leave, on July 4. He was a veteran of nearly two years' service in northeast Mississippi and had had "several turns with Forrest." As Hatch knew the area like a book, he would be a valuable addition, and he was to report to Smith and take command of Coon's cavalry brigade. Reaching La Grange, Hatch told Smith that, after leaving Ripley, the army should advance down the Pontotoc Ridge. When he had last been out this route, there had been large quantities of forage on the farms, and the Federals should have no difficulty feeding their horses and mules as they drove southward.

Washburn was of the opinion that from Pontotoc, Smith's columns should head for Columbus, by way of Okolona. It would be well, he warned, to avoid Tupelo as it was said to be fortified, and make Forrest come out and fight. After reaching Okolona, Smith was to have his people live off the country and conserve their hardtack for the return march.[38]

36 Ibid., 160.

37 Ibid.

38 Ibid., 162.

2

The Confederates Prepare to Strike

GENERAL A. J. Smith on July 4, 1864, alerted his division commanders to have their men formed and ready to march early on the 5th. The infantry and artillery were to be issued three days' rations, while the horse soldiers were to carry rations to last for five days. It would be desirable for the cavalry to take along as much oats for their mounts as possible.[1] Several of the infantry brigade commanders had been shocked by the way their men had straggled on the march from Moscow to La Grange. To prevent a repetition, the company commanders were told to see that each man's canteen was filled with water, before they moved out in the mornings. The promiscuous discharge of small-arms while on the march was forbidden, and regimental and company officers would be held responsible for all violations. The troops were to move out in light marching order, with rubber blankets, and 40 rounds of ammunition in their cartridge-boxes.[2]

Time out from drawing rations and ammunition was taken at noon on the 4th, when a national salute of 100 guns was fired to celebrate the United States' 88th birthday.[3]

1 *O.R.*, Series I, Vol. 39, pt. 2, 163.

2 Ibid.

3 David W. Reed, *Campaigns and Battles of the 12th Regiment Iowa Veteran Volunteer Infantry* (Evanston, 1903), 151.

BRIG. GEN.
BENJAMIN H. GRIERSON

A former music teacher, Grierson was now the senior Federal cavalryman in Mississippi.

Library of Congress

Although the infantry commanders had their brigades formed, mustered, and ready to march by the designated hour on July 5, no orders to move out came. The cavalry was not ready. General Grierson seemed unable to rise to the occasion as he had in April 1863, when he had led the raid from La Grange to Baton Rouge, which dislocated Confederate plans to cope with General Grant's crossing of the Mississippi. It was late in the afternoon before Grierson was able to notify Smith that the cavalry was ready to march. Upon receipt of this anxiously awaited word, Smith passed the word for his infantry to move out. The day was not completely wasted, however, as large fatigue parties had been organized to load aboard railroad cars for return to Lafayette the supplies stockpiled at La Grange and Saulsbury surplus to the army's needs.[4]

After studying his maps and discussing the situation with General Hatch and his scouts, Smith voiced concern that the Rebels might block the road leading down the Pontotoc Ridge from Ripley. If this occurred, he wished to know if he were at liberty to strike for Tuscumbia, Alabama. When General Washburn made no comment on this suggestion, Smith on further reflection concluded that, with Washburn's permission, he would go to "Tuscumbia

4 *O.R.*, Series I, Vol. 39, pt. 2, 165.

and do all the mischief we can on the route," and from there reach Columbus much easier than by way of the Pontotoc Ridge. All were in general agreement, at his headquarters, that an advance via Tuscumbia would: (a) permit the army to live off the country; (b) avoid crossing the Tombigbee; and (c) draw Forrest out if he wanted to fight. As La Grange was a key point in Smith's plan of operations, Hatch, having not yet recovered his strength, would be detailed to hold it with a small force and scout to the south.[5]

Washburn was unimpressed with Smith's proposal. The wily Forrest, he reasoned, would employ his superior mobility to give Smith's army the slip and make a dash into Memphis. Smith's proposal to advance via Tuscumbia was accordingly vetoed.[6]

It was 6 p.m. before Grierson reported his horsesoldiers were ready to mount. Shortly thereafter, Winslow's brigade rode out of Saulsbury, taking the Ripley road. By dusk when the brigade halted and camped, it had advanced seven miles.[7] Grierson's otter brigade, Coon's, was to screen the march of Smith's infantry. Riding out at 6:30, the cavalrymen left La Grange and took the road to Davis's Mill. One of Coon's regiments, the 9th Illinois Cavalry,

5 Ibid., 165.

6 | | In the most recent work covering the campaign, historian Thomas Parson notes that Washburn must have been "stunned" to receive this communique, since it would take Smith's column "an additional hundred miles" eastward, into Alabama, and completely uncovering Memphis should Forrest not take the bait and follow. Parson speculates that Smith might have been angling to get far enough east to avoid having to return to Memphis, but instead rejoin Sherman and that portion of the Army of the Tennessee then fighting outside Atlanta; or alternatively, marching south to threaten Mobile, as proposed by General Canby. Parson, *Work for Giants*, 78.

7 *O.R.*, Series I, Vol. 39, pt. 1, 304, 305, 307, 312, 313. While Winslow's brigade was at Saulsbury, am outpost on the Ripley road manned by Companies D and B, 3d Iowa Cavalry, had been attacked by a Confederate patrol. A sharp clash had ensued which cost the Federals one wounded and the Confederates five casualties. Ibid., 307.

remained behind to cover the army's rear. Nightfall found Coon's troopers halted on Woodson's plantation, five miles southeast of La Grange.[8]

General Joseph Mower, as senior division commander, took the lead as the infantry broke camp. Moore's division came next followed by Bouton's brigade and the army trains. The footsoldiers spent the night at Davis's Mill. Each brigade was accompanied by a train of 26 wagons in which were loaded a reserve of 100 rounds of ammunition per man, nine days' rations for the troops, and nine days' grain and forage for the livestock. General A. J. Smith, accompanied by his staff, rode out of La Grange at dusk and soon overtook the infantry columns. On checking with his assistant adjutant general, he found that his army, as it took the field, mustered 14,000 effectives, supported by 24 field guns.[9]

July 6 found the main column, still spearheaded by Coon's brigade, taking up the march from Davis's Mill toward Ripley. Contact was soon established with Confederate scouts, who retired without delaying the Union advance. The army had closed to within 15 miles of Ripley before Smith called a halt. Meanwhile, back at La Grange the 9th Illinois Cavalry had been relieved by troops from Memphis, and Lt. Col. Henry B. Burgh led his people down the road to Davis's Mill, where they spent the night.[10] Winslow's cavalry brigade, having a shorter distance to march, had

8 Ibid., 315, 316, 317, 318, 319. While at La Grange, the 9th Illinois Cavalry had been reconnoitering south of the railroad. On the 3d a patrol led by Lt. John H. McMahon had skirmished with Confederate scouts.

9 *O.R.*, Series I, Vol. 39, pt. 2, 165; *O.R.*, Ser. I, Vol. 39, pt. 1, 250, 256, 279, 300. In addition to the 9th Illinois Cavalry, the construction train remained in La Grange on the night of July 5. Smith hoped that Washburn would send a force, on the morning of the 6th, to relieve the Illinois regiment. *O.R.*, Series. I, Vol. 39, pt. 2, 165.

10 *O.R.*, Series I, Vol. 39, pt. 1, 315, 317; *History of the 9th Regiment Illinois Cavalry Volunteers, edited by Edward A. Davenport* (Chicago, 1888), 117.

not broken camp until noon. After a short ride, the brigade reached and turned into the La Grange-Ripley road, where it rendezvoused with Coon's brigade, and Winslow reported to General Grierson.[11]

Early the next morning, July 7, the march was renewed with the entire column traveling via the La Grange-Ripley road. In accordance with instructions from General Grierson, Colonel Coon's brigade, with the 2d Iowa Cavalry as advance guard, had the lead. As on the previous day, contact was established with Rebel scouts. Shots were exchanged as the butternuts fell back. By 3 p.m. the 2d Iowa was within three and one-half miles of Ripley, and Colonel Coon, who was riding with the vanguard, found a strong force of Confederates (the 1st Mississippi Partisans and the 3d Tennessee) under Lt. Col. Samuel M. Hyams posted on a hillside, their position partially masked by trees and underbrush. Coon dismounted six companies of the 2d Iowa and attacked. After maneuvering for a position for an hour, during which a great quantity of ammunition was expended, the Iowans charged across an open field and dislodged the Rebels from the hillside. In policing the field, the Iowans found ten dead Confederates. A roll call disclosed that only four bluecoats had been injured in the fighting. By the time the horsesoldiers had secured the field, General Smith had arrived with Mower's lead brigade, and he called a halt for the day, the army camping on North Tippah Creek, three miles northwest of Ripley.[12]

Confederate Maj. Gen. Nathan Bedford Forrest and his cavalry corps were permitted little time to celebrate and exchange mutual congratulations over the defeat of General Sturgis's column. Scouts had sighted and counted the steamboats bringing A. J. Smith's divisions up the

11 *O.R.*, Series I, Vol. 39, pt. 1, 305.

12 *O.R.*, Series I, Vol. 39, pt. 1, 250, 304, 315, 318.

Mississippi, as they passed Austin on June 9. Spies in Memphis and at Byhalia reported on the 10th that 20,000 troops had disembarked, and that a "heavy force reached White's Station on the night of the 11th. Working parties had been spotted on the Memphis & Charleston Railroad as far east as Moscow, putting down new cross-ties. Orders had been issued by the Union military in Memphis exempting all blacksmiths and wagon-makers from military service for six days. Five trains had passed Forest Hill by the 12th going east; two of the trains were carrying horses inside box-cars and men on top; while the others were made up of flat-cars crowded with infantry. Three of the trains had returned, one with only a train guard, one with Sturgis's wounded, while the scouts had been unable to ascertain the character of the command riding the other.

This information reached General Forrest's Tupelo headquarters on June 15. Forrest, satisfied that the Federals were organizing another expedition aimed at the destruction of his corps, relayed this information to his immediate superior, Maj. Gen. Stephen D. Lee, who as commander of the Department of Alabama, Mississippi, and East Louisiana maintained his headquarters at Meridian. On doing so, he suggested that "every preparation should be made to meet the enemy in case they . . . move out."[13]

The urgency abated somewhat when the scouts and spies reported on the 14th that the force sent out from Memphis on the 12th had returned, after meeting Sturgis's shattered command.[14] General Lee, to be prepared for any eventuality, on June 18 directed Brig. Gen. Philip D. Roddey to concentrate his division, except for 350 men of Patterson's brigade, at or near Corinth. Col. Josiah Patterson's people were to remain in north Alabama and keep close watch

13 *O.R.*, Series I, Vol. 39, pt. 2, 651.

14 Ibid., 652.

on the Union garrison holding Decatur. As long as the Federals held Memphis in force, Lee warned, it would make impracticable a raid on the foe's Middle Tennessee supply lines and depots.[15]

Here General Lee demonstrated that he did not have the ability to comprehend the strategic thinking behind the advance of Sherman's "Army Group" toward Atlanta and the activities of the Union forces based at Memphis and Vicksburg. While Sherman was exerting himself to insure the defeat of Forrest's corps to prevent the destruction of his supply line, several high Confederate officers were pleading with the government in Richmond to overrule General Lee and give up north Mississippi. Gen. Joseph E. Johnston, whose Army of Tennessee was endeavoring to halt Sherman's push on Atlanta, twice, on June 13 and again on July 16, suggested to President Jefferson Davis that "an adequate force under the most competent officer in America for such service, General N. B. Forrest be sent to operate against Sherman's communications." He did "so in the confidence that this cavalry would serve the Confederacy far better by insuring the defeat of a great invasion than by

15 Ibid., 655. Roddey commanded the District of North Alabama, with headquarters at Tuscumbia. | | Brig. Gen. Philip D. Roddey was a native of North Alabama. Though he had little formal education, Roddey was a man of many talents; he worked as a tailor, served as county sheriff, and later was involved in steamboating on the Tennessee. With the coming of the war, he raised first a company and later a battalion of cavalry, which grew to a full regiment—the 4th Alabama—in the fall of 1862. He commanded a semi-independent brigade tasked with defending northern Alabama along the south bank of the Tennessee River for much of 1863 and 1864. He proved adept at independent command, ably contesting repeated Union forays despite leading a force that rarely numbered more than 1,500 men at any one time. He ended the war serving under Nathan Bedford Forrest, surrendering his command at Selma in 1865. See William C. Davis, ed., *The Confederate General.* 6 vols. (National Historical Society: 1991), 5: 104-105.

repelling a mere raid."[16] In this suggestion Johnston was backed by two of his three corps commanders. On June 13, Lt. Gen. Leonidas Polk, in the last official dispatch he was to transmit before being killed at Pine Mountain, urged his friend, the President, to unleash Forrest against Sherman's communications. Lt. Gen. William J. Hardee concurred in this plea.[17]

Governor Joseph E. Brown of Georgia, one of Davis's severest critics, addressed a formal request to the President, asking that General Forrest be placed in command of all the cavalry, with the mission of operating with Johnston's Army of Tennessee. His request having been turned down, he telegraphed Davis on June 5, "I regret that you cannot grant my request. I am satisfied that Sherman's escape with his army would be impossible if ten thousand good cavalry under Forrest were thrown in his rear this side of Chattanooga, and his supplies were cut off."[18]

Maj. Gen. Howell Cobb of Georgia in July wrote Secretary of War James A. Seddon, pointing out that the defense of Atlanta and "the certain defeat and destruction of Sherman's army are involved in some movement to be made by Forrest, if possible, on Sherman's line of communication." Unless this were done, Cobb foresaw no end to Sherman's methodical advance into Georgia. If his communications were cut for ten days, he argued, Sherman's "Army Group" would be

16 John A. Wyeth, *Life of Lieutenant-General Nathan Bedford Forrest* (New York, 1899), 432-433; *Battles and Leaders of the Civil War*, edited by Robert U. Johnson and Clarence C. Buel, four vols. (New York, 1885-1887), Vol. 4, 276. During this same period, General Johnston on four other occasions, through Gen. Braxton Bragg, broached the same subject.

17 Robert S. Henry, *"First With the Most" Forrest* (Indianapolis, 1944), 308.

18 Wyeth, *Life of General N. B. Forrest*, 433.

destroyed. "To effect such a result," can we not "afford to uncover for a short time the country protected by Forrest?"[19]

Despite the pleas of Johnston and his generals, reinforced by Governor Brown and General Cobb, President Davis refused to overrule General Lee. Both Davis and Lee were wedded to a policy of holding onto Mississippi, instead of unleashing Forrest's cavalry corps on Sherman's supply line.[20]

Generals Lee and Forrest on the 20th learned from their sources in northwest Mississippi that A. J. Smith, with a considerable force, was still in Memphis. With working parties rebuilding the Memphis & Charleston to La Grange, all signs indicated that they had better be prepared to meet another raid in force.[21] The next day, the 21st, the 2d Missouri Cavalry of Chalmers's division was ordered to take position at Abbeville "to observe the movements of the enemy in that quarter." Scouts would be thrown out toward

19 Ibid., 433-434. | | Howell Cobb was a prominent pre-war Georgia politician who commanded a brigade in the Army of Northern Virginia in 1861 and 1862. After his brigade was routed at the battle of Crampton's Gap in South Mountain on September 14, 1862, Cobb left active field service to take charge of northern Florida. Fifty years of age and considerably overweight, Cobb, who was "once described as a 'fat, pussy, round-faced, jolly-looking fellow,'" was better suited to administrative duties. In 1864 he was assigned to help recruit and organize Georgia's state militia forces to supplement Johnston's main army, with limited success. Cobb and Governor Joseph Brown often clashed over policy and use of these reserves, leaving Cobb frustrated. Davis, *The Confederate General*, 1: 207-208.

20 | | Most other historians agree with Bearss's assessment. In his study of the Confederate high command, Steven Woodworth described the decision to retain Forrest in Mississippi instead of unleashing him on Sherman's supply line as "sheer folly for the Confederacy." Steven E. Woodworth, *Jefferson Davis and his Generals, The Failure of Confederate Command in the West* (Lawrence, KS: 1990), 278. Albert Castel, in his monumental study of the Atlanta Campaign, argued that keeping Forrest in Mississippi and away from Sherman's logistical lifeline was "the essential thing." Albert Castel, *Decision in the West, The Atlanta Campaign of 1864* (Lawrence, KS: 1992), 278.

21 *O.R.*, Series I, Vol. 39, pt. 2, 659.

MAJ. GEN. NATHAN BEDFORD FORREST

One of the finest cavalry commanders of the war.

Library of Congress

Memphis and keep the Memphis & Charleston under observation. If the foe advanced, the Missourians were to harass him, and if compelled to retire they would rejoin the division.[22]

On June 22 General Lee warned Richmond that A. J. Smith was outfitting at Memphis "a formidable expedition . . . to repair the disaster of General Sturgis." Reports placed the strength of the Union force at Memphis and

22 Ibid., 657. There was a telegraph in operation linking Holly Springs with Chalmers's headquarters in Aberdeen.

along the Memphis & Charleston at 20,000. Forrest had 9,000 horsesoldiers available with which to meet Smith's columns, and Lee promised that "every effort will be made to meet this force."[23]

President Davis, when shown Lee's communication, fumed. He urged that steps be taken by Lee to concentrate a force for the defense of his department and for raids on the supply lines and depots used to support Sherman's "Army Group." While the redeployment of General Polk's two infantry divisions to Georgia had been authorized, it had been done on the supposition that General Johnston would fight Sherman at or near Dalton, "so as to relieve the danger to Alabama and Mississippi." Now, however, the retreat of the Army of Tennessee had exposed the country Polk was charged with protecting. In addition, the War Department had not sanctioned the transfer of Brig. Gen. William H. Jackson's cavalry division from Mississippi to northwestern Georgia. The President wanted Lee to keep in hand all the force he had left, including Brig. Gens. Philip D. Roddey's and Gideon Pillow's, and General Johnston was to be notified that "he may not count on aid from General Lee, but rather perceive that the drafts upon the Department of Alabama, Mississippi, and East Louisiana have been already too great."[24]

To insure a rapid concentration to oppose Smith's advance, Lee contacted his commander at Jackson, Brig. Gen. William Wirt Adams. Adams was to move Brig. Gen. Samuel Gholson's brigade to West, leaving 500 men to cover the line of the Big Black toward Vicksburg. One-half of Col. John S. Scott's brigade was to be pulled out of east Louisiana and take station at Brookhaven. Lee wanted Adams's

23 Ibid., 657-658; Stephen D. Lee, "The Battle of Tupelo," *Publications of the Mississippi Historical Society* (Oxford, 1902), Vol. 6, 41.

24 *O.R.*, Series I, Vol. 39, pt. 2, 658. Pillow's small cavalry division was currently operating in northeast Alabama.

command to be ready to move into north Mississippi, and still have "a sufficient force within striking distance of the Vicksburg front." Adams for the time being was to remain at Jackson, but he and his staff were to hold themselves ready to join the army in northeast Mississippi if called.[25]

Lee on the 23d learned from Adams's scouts that the Federals had materially strengthened their force at Vicksburg. Two thousand soldiers had returned to duty at the expiration of their re-enlistment furloughs. Five white regiments and 2,000 Negro soldiers were reported to have reached Vicksburg by boat from Morganza.[26] If these soldiers were to undertake an expedition from Vicksburg toward Jackson or Yazoo City, Lee would find himself hard-pressed to locate sufficient men to meet it, while concentrating against A. J. Smith.[27]

General Forrest on the 25th received a number of interesting reports from his scouts. Men posted 24 miles east of Memphis had counted 184 wagons and 20 ambulances as they rolled past Forest Hill. They estimated that 12,000 troops had passed. Forrest, knowing that scouts were likely to exaggerate, was inclined to scale down this figure. At the same time, he estimated that when A. J. Smith did take the

25 Ibid., 659-660. | | William Wirt Adams, a Kentuckian by birth, had served in the Army of the Republic of Texas, and subsequently, been a planter, banker, and politician in Mississippi. In the summer of 1864, he commanded a cavalry division in the District of Southern Mississippi and East Louisiana, under S. D. Lee. His brigade commanders were Cols. Hinchie P. Mabry, of the 3rd Texas Cavalry, and John L. Scott of the 1st Louisiana. Gholson's brigade acted semi-independently, serving under both Adams and Forrest that summer. See Warner, *Generals in Gray*, 2-3; Steven H. Newton, *Lost for the Cause, The Confederate Army in 1864*, 288.

26 There was no truth to the story telling of the arrival at Vicksburg of the troops from Morganza.

27 Ibid., 660. On the 23d Lee was promoted to lieutenant general and named to command of the Department of Alabama, Mississippi, and East Louisiana, to replace General Polk who had been killed by Union artillery fire at Pine Mountain, Georgia, on June 14. Ibid.

field, he would move with 18,000 to 20,000, "a portion of which will be used to garrison the points already fortified" on the railroad. Smith's column, he warned his superiors, had for its goal the destruction of the Mobile & Ohio Railroad as far south as possible, and when it returned to its base it would do so by way of the Mississippi Central Railroad.

To be prepared for this movement, all surplus stores stockpiled in depots and magazines at Grenada and other points on the latter railroad farther north were to be moved toward Meridian. Besides three companies of scouts, Forrest had 200 men at Ripley, and he had alerted his brother, Lt. Col. Jesse Forrest, to take another 200 troopers of Bell's and Lyon's brigades and penetrate as close to La Grange as possible. These men were to watch the roads and ascertain what the 3,000 Federals at La Grange were doing. Forrest would have sent out a stronger force, "but for the difficulty of supplying it with forage, not having a sufficiency of mules."[28]

Orders were issued at this time by Forrest for Brig. Gen. James R. Chalmers to bring his division from its rest camp at Aberdeen to "as near Okolona as nature of forage will permit." Steps would then be taken to ready the division for the field by supplying each man with five days' rations and 100 rounds of snail-arms ammunition. As the Federal build-up was proceeding slowly and methodically, Chalmers would not be required to make a forced march. Forrest at the same time suggested that Lee call up Col. Hinchie P. Mabry's brigade of General Wirt Adams's command to reinforce the force he was concentrating along the Mobile

28 Ibid., 666; R. R. Hancock, *Hancock's Diary: or, A History of the Second Tennessee Cavalry* (Nashville, 1887), 410.

& Ohio.[29] Lee did as Forrest asked, and Mabry's brigade rode from the Yazoo country to Okolona.[30]

General Forrest on the 27th learned from his scouts that Grierson's cavalry had reached Saulsbury, while Smith's infantry was camped in and around La Grange. Confederate spies had penetrated Smith's camps and gauged his strength, which they placed at eight infantry brigades and 3,500 cavalry. His people having torn up the track east of Saulsbury, Forrest felt that Smith would have to cut loose from the railroad at that point.[31]

General Lee, after evaluating the information forwarded by Forrest, telegraphed the War Department on the 28th that Smith's expedition would probably start from Saulsbury within six days. From the cars with which it was being organized, it would be more than a raid and fears were voiced that Selma, Alabama, or a junction with Sherman in Georgia was its goal. A column also was being organized at Vicksburg to support Smith's thrust.[32]

On Tuesday, June 28, Forrest checked with Roddey and Mabry, and he was cheered to learn that their combined commands numbered about 6,000 effectives. Chalmers, who had moved his division to Verona, was told to have his troopers ready to take the field on Thursday, at 6 a.m., with four days' cooked rations for the men and two days' forage for their mounts. Each man was to have 40 rounds of ammunition in his cartridge-box and a reserve of 60

29 *O.R.*, Series I, Vol. 39, pt. 2, 665, 666, 667.

30 Ibid., 671; Henry, *"First With the Most,"* 311. | | Mabry was a pre-war lawyer before enlisting in the 3rd Texas Cavalry. According to the handbook of Texas, Mabry "quickly established a reputation for audacity, courage, and strict discipline." He was assigned to command his current brigade of mixed Arkansas and Mississippi troops in March 1864. https://www.tshaonline.org/handbook/entries/mabry-hinche-parham, accessed 7/17/2021.

31 *O.R.*, Series I, Vol. 39, pt. 2, 668, 670.

32 Ibid., 670; Lee, "Battle of Tupelo," *Publications*, Vol. 6, 41.

rounds in the ordnance wagons. There would be 30 rounds for each pistol, ten to be issued and the remainder held in the wagons. The commissary department was to issue to the division five days' rations of hardtack and bacon.[33] Chalmers was to organize his dismounted men into companies under competent officers and send them to Tupelo.[34]

Forrest had established at Tupelo a camp for men who had lost their horses, or whose mounts did not pass a rigid inspection designed to winnow out "all horses unable to stand the fatigues of service." The purpose was to avoid the "loss of the service of both man and horse," to cut down "straggling and scattering men along the line of march," to "recruit horses that a few days' service at this time would render worthless," and while accomplishing all these desirable ends, to get from the temporarily dismounted men the equivalent of a "good brigade of infantry." At first, some of the men "ran away rather than come to the dismounted camp," although most of them—between 500 and 600—"once in camp and assured of the design to recruit their stock and render it serviceable," appeared satisfied.

To these dismounted men, Forrest purposed to add, by rigid examination, a large number of "attaches, employees, and detailed men," provost guards, purchasing agents, presumed officers of the state reserves between 18 and 45, and others whom, he felt, would bring up his dismounted force to at least 2,000 officers and men. Many of these "exempts" of various sorts were beyond Forrest's reach, but his own detailed men were to be armed with "guns and necessary accoutrements to go into the fight," and

33 *O.R.*, Series I, Vol. 39, pt. 1, 671-672.

34 Ibid., 672, 674. The dismounted men were to be armed with either Enfield or Austrian rifle-muskets.

subordinate commanders were to be held accountable to see that they did.[35]

In the afternoon Forrest left Tupelo for Corinth to inspect Roddey's division. Before doing so, be telegraphed his congratulations to Lee on his promotion to lieutenant general. As Forrest was suffering from boils, he hoped Lee would take command when and if Smith moved out. "Our force," he warned, "is insufficient" to engage the foe, unless reinforcements are forthcoming.[36] Capt. John W. Morton of the artillery recalled that as he left for Corinth, Forrest's keen suffering "depleted even his iron constitution," but, boils or no boils, there was to be no rest and no relief for him. The pressure on the department, with other expeditions threatening from Vicksburg and Morganza, was such that Lee could not dispense with Forrest for even a few days.[37]

Forrest on June 30 was back in Tupelo, where he alerted Chalmers to hold two regiments (the 3d and 7th Tennessee) ready to ride at an hour's notice.[38] Reports now reached Tupelo from Col. Jesse Forrest at Ripley, stating that the Federals were staying close to their camps at La Grange and Saulsbury and continuing their build-up. Instructions were accordingly issued for Chalmers to forget about sending the two regiments to the front. On July 3 Forrest determined to strengthen the force guarding the approaches to Ripley. The 1st Mississippi Partisan Rangers, a unit raised in the region and familiar with all the roads and byways, rode out of Tupelo. At Ripley, Lt. Col. Samuel M. Hyams, as senior officer, took charge and reinforced the

35 Thomas Jordan & J. P. Pryor, *The Campaigns of Lieut-Gen. N. B. Forrest* (New Orleans, 1868), 496; *O.R.*, Series I, Vol. 39, pt. 2, 682-684; Henry, *"First with the Most,"* 312.

36 *O.R.*, Series I, Vol. 39, pt. 2, 671.

37 John W. Morton, *The Artillery of Nathan Bedford Forrest's Cavalry* (Nashville, 1909), 203.

38 *O.R.*, Series I, Vol. 39, pt. 2, 675.

patrols Colonel Forrest had posted to the front to watch the Federals' movements. All information gathered was relayed to corps headquarters at Tupelo.[39]

News that the Federals had broken camp and were advancing toward Ripley reached Tupelo on July 6. General Forrest thereupon issued orders for his division and brigade commanders to see that three days' rations were prepared for their commands and that they were ready to move by 6 a.m. on the 7th.[40] Reports arriving from Colonel Hyams at Ripley on the 7th satisfied Forrest that the Yankees were striking for Tupelo by way of Ellistown. Orders were issued for Brig. Gen. Abraham Buford to send a brigade, Col. Tyree H. Bell's, to watch the Ellistown-Ripley road. At 5 a.m. on July 8, Bell's Tennesseans rode out of their camp, three miles northwest of Tupelo. Bell, on reaching Ellistown, halted the 2d and 16th Tennessee, while he with his other regiments (the 15th Tennessee and Newsom's) pushed on to the Tallahatchie, where they took position picketing the crossings. The next morning, the 9th, the 2d Tennessee was advanced toward New Albany, the 16th remaining at Ellistown as a ready reserve.[41]

General Forrest on July 8 learned of the fight at Ripley between Hyams's command and Smith's vanguard, and that the Federals had passed through Ripley and were pressing deeper into Mississippi. Instructions were now issued alerting his three division commanders—Chalmers, Buford, and Roddey—to hold their units "in readiness for a move at a moment's notice." Chalmers was to send several

39 Ibid., 681-682. The Mississippians carried with them on their horses three days' cooked rations and two days' forage. Three days' rations and four days' corn in sacks, along with an additional 40 round of ammunition per man, was transported to Ripley in wagons. The corn had been sacked by the Tupelo quartermaster.

40 Ibid., 689; *O.R.*, Series I, Vol. 39, pt. 1, 329; Hancock, *Diary*, 411-412.

41 *O.R.*, Series I, Vol. 39, pt. 1, 346; Hancock, *Diary*, 411-412.

good officers "to examine the roads, creeks, and crossings on the New Albany road."[42]

General Lee had reached Tupelo on the 7th by rail from Meridian with 600 heavy artillerists converted into infantry, commanded by Lt. Col. Daniel Beltzhoover, who had been stationed at Mobile.[43] The trains that brought up the reinforcements were used to send the corps' tents and superfluous gear south.[44] Besides worrying about Smith's army and the advance of the Vicksburg Federals on Jackson, Lee had to think about the defense of Mobile. To hold that vital point, which guarded the entrance to mighty rivers penetrating deep into his department, Lee had about 2,500 infantry under Maj. Gen. Dabney H. Maury and a small fleet commanded by Rear Admiral Franklin Buchanan. When he caught the train for Tupelo, Lee knew that a powerful Union fleet under Rear Admiral David G. Farragut was blockading the entrance to Mobile Bay, while his spies in New Orleans were reporting that General Canby was organizing an army of 20,000 men to put ashore at Pascagoula and attack Mobile by land.[45]

Examining Forrest's returns, Lee found that he had assembled an army of 7,500 cavalry, 2,100 dismounted men, and 20 cannon with which to oppose Smith's columns.

42 *O.R.*, Series I, Vol. 39, pt. 2, 694-695.

43 | | Lieutenant Colonel Daniel Beltzhoover, a West Point graduate, class of 1837, joined the Confederate army as an artillery battery commander in 1861. By 1864, he was teaching at the newly established "School of Practice for Artillerists" in Mobile, Alabama, the brainchild of Maj. Gen. Dabney M. Maury. The school had been in session since May when the class was activated for emergency field service under Beltzhoover's command. See John A. Miller, "Lieutenant Colonel Daniel Beltzhoover, CSA, A Mount Saint Mary's College Professor," at https://www.emmitsburg.net/archive_list/articles/history/civil_war/belzhoover.htm, accessed 7/17/2021.

44 Hancock, *Diary*, 411.

45 Lee, "The Battle of Tupelo," *Publications*, Vol. 6, 41-42; *O.R.*, Series I, Vol. 39, pt. 2, 693.

Between them, Lee and Forrest determined to lure Smith as far south as Okolona before attacking. This plan was predicated by the necessity to be in position to rapidly shuttle troops to Mobile by rail in case of an attack on that city by Canby's army. Negroes were impressed and put to work throwing up rifle-pits and artillery emplacements covering the approaches to Okolona.[46]

General A. J. Smith's columns continued their advance on July 8. Smith was careful not to repeat Sturgis's error of permitting his column to be attacked while it was in motion, and to be doubled up and defeated before he could form his infantry into lines of battle. When the army broke camp at daybreak on the 8th, General Grierson told Colonel Winslow to take the advance. Spearheaded by the 10th Missouri Cavalry, Winslow's people rode through Ripley and turned into the New Albany road. There was slight skirmishing between the Missourians and Colonel Hyams's rear guard as the Federals closed in on Orizaba.

Grierson, to confuse the Confederates as to Smith's intentions, now told Winslow to detach one of his regiments for a forced reconnaissance down the Ellistown road to Kelly's Mill. The 3d Iowa Cavalry was given this mission. A one-half mile advance brought the Iowans up before a formidable breastwork on the brow of a hill. The Confederates, seeing that they were outnumbered and had been outflanked by the march of the main column, abandoned their position and retired across the Tallahatchie at Kelly's Ford. As the Iowans pushed on, they saw that the road, as well as the side roads, had been heavily traveled. Satisfied that the Rebels held Kelly's Ford in strength, Col. John W. Noble, after an advance of four miles, called a halt and countermarched his regiment. There were skirmishes as Confederate patrols closed in on the Iowans' flanks. By the time the 3d Iowa

46 Lee, "The Battle of Tupelo," *Publications*, Vol. 6, 42.

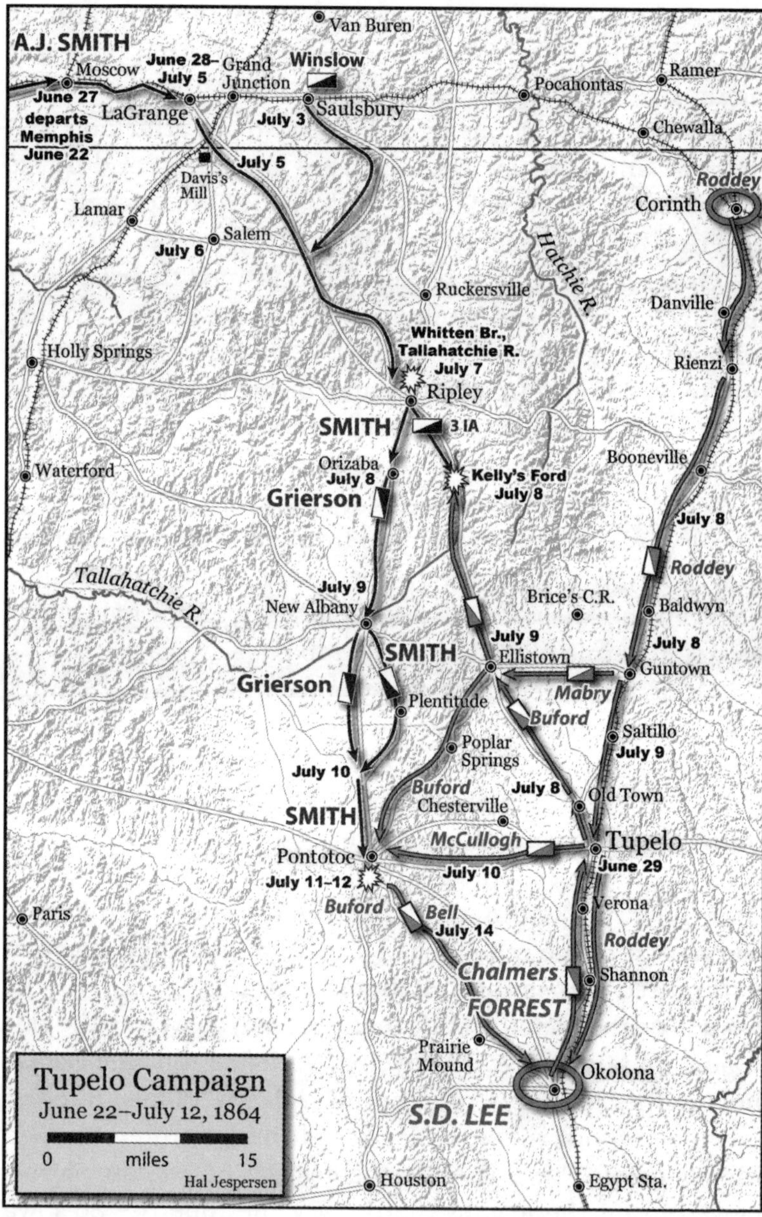
A.J. SMITH
Van Buren
Moscow
June 28–July 5
Grand Junction
Winslow
June 27
departs Memphis June 22
LaGrange
July 3
Saulsbury
Pocahontas
Ramer
Chewalla
July 5
Davis's Mill
Roddey
Corinth
Lamar
Salem
July 6
Hatchie R.
Ruckersville
Danville
Whitten Br., Tallahatchie R.
July 7
Holly Springs
Rienzi
Ripley
SMITH
3 IA
Orizaba
July 8
Waterford
Booneville
Kelly's Ford
July 8
Grierson
July 8
Roddey
Tallahatchie R.
July 9
New Albany
Brice's C.R.
Baldwyn
July 9
July 8
SMITH
Ellistown
Guntown
Grierson
Plentitude
Mabry
Buford
Poplar Springs
Saltillo
July 9
July 10
Buford
July 8
Old Town
SMITH
Chesterville
McCullogh
Tupelo
Pontotoc
July 10
June 29
July 11–12
Verona
Paris
Buford
Bell
July 14
Roddey
Chalmers
Shannon
FORREST
Prairie Mound
Okolona
S.D. LEE
Houston
Egypt Sta.
Tupelo Campaign
June 22–July 12, 1864
0 miles 15
Hal Jespersen

Brig. Gen. A. J. Smith's careful, deliberate movements south from his depot at LaGrange were aimed at drawing Confederate cavalryman Nathan Bedford Forrest out from behind what was presumed to be a fortified camp at Tupelo. In response, Forrest and Maj. Gen. Stephen D. Lee rushed to concentrate their forces at Okolona.

---

rejoined the army on the evening of July 8, it had gone into camp one mile south of Orizaba.[47]

Ripley had suffered at the hands of the Federals. Pursuant to instructions for the punishment of Forrest and the people, much of the village—the Tippah County Courthouse, the Methodist and Presbyterian churches, the Masonic and Odd Fellows Hall, and a number of dwellings—were burned, before the rearguard had turned into the New Albany road. As the army pushed on toward Orizaba, a swath of desolation ten miles across was left.[48]

General Grierson rotated his brigades, so it was Coon's turn to take the advance on the 9th. The march was uneventful with no significant contacts with Confederates reported by the patrols sent out by Colonel Coon. Generals A. J. Smith and Grierson were delighted when the horsesoldiers made an unopposed crossing of the Tallahatchie at Williamson's Mill. By nightfall the Federals were south of the Tallahatchie and bivouacked in and around New Albany.[49]

The 2d Tennessee, Col. Clark Barteau commanding, was detached by Colonel Bell on the 9th and rode westward from Ellistown. Barteau was under orders to establish a roadblock on the New Albany-Pontotoc road. Barteau, on reaching the road, deployed his wen in line of battle, six stiles south of New Albany, and waited.[50]

47 *O.R.*, Series I, Vol. 39, pt. 1, 304, 306, 308.

48 Henry, *"First with the Most,"* 314.

49 *O.R.*, Series I, Vol. 39, pt. 1, 306.

50 Hancock, *Diary*, 412.

Meanwhile, General Buford, accompanied by Brig. Gen. Hylan B. Lyon's brigade, had left Tupelo, taking the Ellistown road. At Ellistown, Buford was reinforced by Mabry's brigade, which had ridden over from Saltillo.[51] Buford now learned from Colonel Bell that the foe had changed his line of march, abandoning the Ripley-Ellistown road in favor of the road passing down the Pontotoc ridge. Bell explained to his superior that he had sent the 2d Tennessee to delay Smith's advance, so the Confederates, if they moved promptly, could reach Pontotoc first. Buford nodded approval and prepared to intercept Smith's army. Before starting for Pontotoc, Buford had Mabry detach Col. Isham Harrison's 6th Mississippi Cavalry. Harrison's people were to take position on the road to Plentitude and operate on the flank and rear of the Federal column as it advanced down the Pontotoc Ridge.[52]

Buford, to make up for lost time, kept his men in the saddle all night, and at daybreak they halted two miles east of Pontotoc. Here Buford received orders from General Forrest directing him "to develop the enemy's strength, not to bring on a general engagement, but keep in the enemy's front and on his flanks and gradually fall back to Okolona."[53] Buford felt that with the 6th Mississippi at Plentitude and the 2d Tennessee on the New Albany road he had divined Forrest's wishes. At 7:30 a.m. a courier galloped in from Tupelo with a message from Forrest to post the division on the Chesterville road, "join the command at Okolona, and to send a squadron of 100 good men in rear of the enemy to cut off his communications."[54]

51 Mabry's brigade, during the first week of July, had been transferred from Okolona to Saltillo.

52 *O.R.*, Series I, Vol. 39, pt. 1, 320, 329, 338, 341, 342, 346, 348. Bell's brigade, less the 2d Tennessee, would accompany the division to Pontotoc.

53 Ibid., 320, 329.

54 Ibid., 329.

BRIG. GEN.
ABRAHAM BUFORD
A West Pointer of the class of 1841 from Woodford County Kentucky, Buford was one of Forrest's principal subordinates.

Library of Congress

In accordance with Forrest's orders, Buford called on the commander of Faulkner's Kentucky Regiment to detail 100 picked men. Captain H. A. Tyler with the 100 volunteers rode out of Pontotoc on the King's Ferry road. During the day, the 10th, Tyler's people encountered and drove in two patrols sent by General Grierson to investigate the area west of the Union line of advance.[55]

Forrest, late on July 9, learned from his spies that the foe had crossed the Tallahatchie and had occupied New Albany. Marching orders were forwarded to Chalmers and Roddey. The latter officer was to hasten by forced marches, night and day, from Corinth to Okolona. Chalmers was to send one brigade (Rucker's) to the camp of the dismounted brigade and to throw out scouts toward Chesterville and Pontotoc. Col. Robert McCulloch's brigade was to be rushed to Pontotoc, while the division trains were driven to Garvin's Mills on the Okolona road.[56]

It was 11 p.m. when a copy of Forrest's dispatch was handed to Chalmers at his Verona headquarters. Till this

55 Ibid., 344.

56 *O.R.*, Series I, Vol. 39, pt. 2, 696; Hancock, *Diary*, 412. The infantry camp was four miles west of Tupelo at the intersection of the Tupelo-Pontotoc and Chesterville-Okolona roads. *O.R.*, Series I, Vol. 39, pt. 1, 324.

hour he had received no reports from the scouts ordered out on the previous day, so he was ignorant as to "the strength, position, or movements of the enemy." Calling for his brigade commanders, Chalmers told McCulloch to start his horsesoldiers for Pontotoc, while Col. Edmund Rucker's rode from Verona to the infantry encampment. Maj. B. S. Crump was told to gallop up the road to Tupelo and ask Forrest for additional instructions. Crump returned at daybreak on the 10th with orders for Chalmers to join Buford and to assume field command of the two divisions. With this force he was to "skirmish with the enemy, and make him develop his strength, but not to bring on a general engagement."[57]

McCulloch's brigade in the meantime had marched from Verona to Pontotoc, where it reported to Buford at 9 a.m. In compliance with Forrest's instructions of the previous evening to rendezvous at Okolona, Buford at 1 p.m. ordered his men to mount, and they rode down the Okolona road about six miles. Here Buford called a halt and posted Mabry's and Lyon's brigades in a strong position behind Chiwapa Creek. Bell's brigade had exhausted its forage, so it proceeded to Okolona, where the quartermaster had several warehouses full of corn. McCulloch's brigade remained in Pontotoc to support the 2d Tennessee Cavalry manning the roadblock north of Cherry Creek. This was familiar country for the Confederates, because it was along the Pontotoc-Okolona road that they had mauled Union Brig. Gen. W. S. Sooy Smith's column in February 1864.[58]

General Chalmers, because of these movements, experienced difficulty in locating Buford's command post. It was after dark on July 10 before the two generals met. From Buford, Chalmers learned that "the enemy was moving

57 *O.R.*, Series I, Vol. 39, pt. 1, 324-325.

58 Ibid., 320-321, 325, 329, 346, 348.

very slowly, and usually with a line of battle and skirmishers about one mile in length." Unless they were authorized to employ artillery, it would be impossible to compel the Federals to show their strength. He was also disappointed to learn that Buford, in obedience to Forrest's orders, had sent Bell's brigade and a section of artillery to Okolona. Chalmers notified Forrest of the situation.[59]

General A. J. Smith, realizing that the Rebels were massing to his front, expected to encounter serious resistance on July 10. His army would therefore advance as far as Cherry Creek via parallel roads. Grierson's horsesoldiers were to take the Pontotoc road, while the infantry divisions used the Plentitude road. The country was level and the columns would be within easy supporting distance. It was almost 9 o'clock before the Federals broke camp and started southward from New Albany.

Winslow's brigade took the lead, as Grierson's division swung into the saddle. The day was hot and humid. Lt. Col. John H. Peters and his 4th Iowa Cavalry had the advance. Confederate Colonel Barteau of the 2d Tennessee had roused his men and had them in the saddle before daybreak. Peters and his Iowans encountered Barteau and his people posted on a commanding ridge. He deployed his regiment to the left and right of the Pontotoc road and forced the Rebels to abandon their roadblock. Barteau now divided his regiment into detachments of one or two companies each. These units were positioned astride the road at strategic points, extending back toward Pontotoc. As the foe advanced, the first line would fire, fall back, and form in the rear, then the second would do likewise. These tactics delayed the Federals and sapped the Iowans' energy. Colonel Winslow, seeing that the troopers of the 4th Iowa had been exhausted by the fight, sent the 3d Iowa to their relief. Colonel Noble

59 Ibid., 325, 329-330.

employed Companies I and M as his advance guard, and the 3d Iowa drove forward to Cherry Creek, where the Pontotoc and Plentitude roads converged. The 6th Mississippi Cavalry, which was guarding the Plentitude road, had abandoned its position without a fight, and Smith's infantry had had an easy march. As soon as the footsoldiers reached Cherry Creek, Smith formed them into lines of battle and camped.[60]

After the Union army had halted on Cherry Creek, Barteau recalled his Tennesseans and headed for Pontotoc, where he was relieved by McCulloch's brigade. The 2d Tennessee then rode through Pontotoc and bivouacked five miles east of town on the Tupelo road.[61]

The Union generals had their men fed and in ranks early on the 11th. Colonel Coon's brigade took the lead as the cavalry forded Cherry Creek. The army would march via the Pontotoc road, and the officers were told to keep their men closed up and ready to deploy on a moment's notice, as they "were tramping on the land of Forrest, and a little of that carelessness shown by Sturgis might give us another" Brices Crossroads disaster. The day was hot, and sunstrokes were numerous. Confederate troopers of McCulloch's brigade kept a discreet distance as the Federals marched toward Pontotoc. As Coon's vanguard, the 7th Kansas Cavalry, neared the town, McCulloch's brigade was sighted posted in and around Pontotoc, with its reserve massed on a hill to the south. The 7th Kansas skirmished with the Rebels, while Grierson turned the rest

60 Ibid., 306, 308, 312, 315; Scott, *Story of a Cavalry Regiment*, 285; Hancock, *Diary*, 412-413. Winslow, during the day, had detached the 10th Missouri Cavalry and sent it in pursuit of a Confederate patrol which had broken contact with the 4th Iowa and had moved off to the east. Gaining the Tuscumbia-Pontotoc road, the Missourians sighted a Confederate column, the 6th Mississippi Cavalry, riding toward Pontotoc. The Missourians, having secured this information, reported back to Winslow. *O.R.*, Series I, Vol. 39, pt. 1, 313.

61 Hancock, *Diary*, 413.

of his division into little frequented byways and closed in on Pontotoc from the east. General Mower at the same time reinforced the 7th Kansas with his lead brigade—Col. William L. McMillan's. The footsoldiers were formed into line of battle with their left flank anchored on the road. Colonel McCulloch, in view of orders not to bring on a fight and seeing that he was hopelessly outnumbered, called up his horseholders. Remounting, the Confederates evacuated Pontotoc and retired down the Okolona Stage Road. The Federal cavalry followed the Rebels for several miles, before Grierson called off the pursuit.[62]

General Chalmers, late on the afternoon of July 11, had Lyon's brigade relieve McCulloch's on the Okolona Stage Road, southeast of Pontotoc. Lyon dismounted his Kentuckians and posted them in a strong position behind fence rail and log breastworks on Pinson's Hill. Mabry's brigade would support Lyon's. Satisfied that Lyon's people could hold the roadblock, Chalmers, to cover the other roads radiating out from Pontotoc, had Barteau's 2d Tennessee on the Tupelo road, and Rucker's brigade on the Cotton Gin road. Rucker was to be ready to reinforce Barteau "if necessary without awaiting further orders." McCulloch's brigade was stationed on the Houston road. Forrest was advised of these dispositions, which Chalmers felt would prevent the foe from "moving on in any direction without my knowledge."[63]

Forrest, on learning of Chalmers's deployment, gave his approval, and urged his subordinate to hold the Federals in check for an additional 48 hours, so General Lee could

62 *O.R.*, Series I, Vol. 39, pt. 1, 250, 259, 304, 306, 315, 325, 330; Scott, *Story of the 32d Iowa*, 291.

63 *O.R.*, Series I, Vol. 39, pt. 1, 321, 325; Hancock, *Diary*, 414; J. P. Young, *The Seventh Tennessee Cavalry, Confederate, A History* (Nashville, 1890), 96. Shortly before sunset, Barteau recalled his regiment and moved eastward, camping within three miles of Verona.

complete his preparations to receive Smith's columns near Okolona. The 2d Tennessee was to brace itself for a raid on the Union rear.[64]

Captain Tyler's combat patrol earlier in the day had succeeded in gaining Smith's rear north of Cherry Creek. Tyler's Kentuckians shadowed the bluecoats to within five miles of Pontotoc before striking. Unable to disconcert the vigilant Federal infantry, Tyler rode cross-country to the Tuscumbia-Pontotoc road and closed in on Grierson's rear. When within three miles of Pontotoc, the Confederates were attacked and driven back by a Union patrol from Winslow's brigade. Undaunted, Tyler now struck out for the Tupelo road, which he found had been uncovered by the withdrawal of the 2d Tennessee. Tyler's battalion spent the night on the Tupelo road, six miles east of Pontotoc.[65]

Smith's infantry and Grierson's cavalry on the night of July 11 camped on the hills south of Pontotoc. The 9th Illinois Cavalry, which was armed with seven-shot repeating Spencer carbines, picketed the Okolona Stage Road, one and one-half miles southeast of town. A brigade of infantry and an artillery battery were posted nearby. The picket line covering the footsoldiers' camps was manned by a battalion of the 2d Iowa Cavalry.

The seven-day march under the "hottest sun and in the deepest dust" the veteran bluecoats had encountered in three years of hard campaigning had taken its toll. Many men had collapsed from sunstroke. Several of the more recently organized regiments had been unable to stand the pace, and their men were permitted to drop out of ranks and straggle along as best they could in the cool of the evening. The historian of the 12th Iowa bragged that his unit "made a record of greatest endurance, by bringing

64 *O.R.*, Series I, Vol. 39, pt. 1, 321, 325.

65 Ibid., 344.

more men to camp each night and in better order than any other regiment in the command."[66]

A. J. Smith on July 12 determined to send two combat patrols to feel for the foe. The 9th Illinois Cavalry, supported by the 52d Indiana, would operate on the Okolona Stage Road and the 3d Iowa cavalry on the Houston road. As soon as they were relieved by Coon's brigade, the 9th Illinois started forward. Contact was soon established with Rebel pickets posted in a log cabin. These men of the 14th Confederate were dislodged from their stronghold and retired on Lyon's Pinson's Hill roadblock. Alerted by the shouts and shots, General Lyon saw that his men took cover behind their barricades. To guard Lyon's left, Colonel Mabry called up the 4th Mississippi Cavalry and posted the 38th Mississippi Mounted Infantry in close supporting distance of the roadblock.

Colonel Burgh halted his Illinois horsesoldiers on the ridge overlooking Chiwapa Creek, from where he studied Lyon's position through his field glasses. He observed that the Rebels had carefully selected their ground. The breastworks on Pinson's Hill commanded the swampy bottom, which was about one and one-half miles across. One of the Yanks recalled:

> Just beyond the dense thicket (through which they had just passed] was a large open field, the edge of which was only ten or fifteen rods from our line; around the edge of the field, close to the thicket, extended a rail fence....The fence had been permitted to remain unmolested, while rails were brought from a distance part to render it bullet proof.

As soon as his men had reloaded their Spencers, Colonel Burgh waved Capt. Henry M. Buel's battalion forward.

66 Ibid., 315; Scott, *Story of a Cavalry Regiment*, 285; Reed, *Campaigns & Battles*, 151; *History of the 9th Illinois Cavalry*, 117.

Lyon's Rebels held their fire until the Federals were very close. The volley ripped into the bluecoats with telling effect. Private Jesse Hawes of Company I, 9th Illinois, was within an arm's length of the barricade, when he heard a dozen voices shout, "Don't shoot him!" A big, burly Kentuckian reached over the breastworks and dragged him in. Seeing that his battalion was outnumbered, Hawes told the Confederates that a brigade of infantry was close at hand, and would in short order charge the barricade. This caused Lyon's Kentuckians to remain where they were instead of making a sortie, and Buel was able to withdraw his battalion. Colonel Burgh, having lost 30 men, had seen enough to tell him that the Rebels were in force on the Okolona Stage Road. As soon as the 52d Indiana came up, Colonel Burgh retraced his route and notified Grierson of his repulse.[67]

General Grierson had accompanied the 3d Iowa as it advanced down the Houston road. A short distance beyond the picket line, the vanguard was fired on by men of Willis's Texas Battalion. The Texans had been posted by Colonel McCulloch on a commanding hill. While Grierson watched, Colonel Noble dismounted and deployed a battalion on the right of the road. Covered by the fire of the battalion, the remainder of the regiment stormed across Calloway Creek and up the hill. The torrid weather and rugged terrain sapped the men's vigor, but they were not to be denied and they dislodged the Texans. Grierson ordered the hill held by a battalion, while the regiment advanced and gained a plantation road connecting the Houston and Okolona roads. Noble turned his column into this by-road. As the Iowans approached the Okolona Stage Road, they came under fire from Lyon's Confederates posted on Pinson's Hill. Noble dismounted his men and prepared to attack, but before he could do so, General Grierson ordered him "to cross

67 *O.R.*, Series I, Vol. 39, pt. 1, 250-251, 304, 306, 315, 317, 325, 342, 349; *History of the 9th Illinois Cavalry*, 118-120.

the Okolona road" by his left flank. Upon carrying out this mission, the regiment returned to camp.[68]

Meanwhile, Union scouts had advanced five miles out the Tupelo road. There they encountered a roadblock manned by the 8th Mississippi of Rucker's brigade. The Mississippians easily turned back the Federals.[69]

During the afternoon there was excitement in the camps of the Union infantry southeast of Pontotoc. About 2 p.m. a Confederate patrol approached the camp of Bouton's brigade and fired on some soldiers of the 59th U. S. Colored Troops picking berries. While the soldiers scattered, Colonel Bouton had the "Long Roll" beaten and sent Company C, 59th U. S. Colored Troops, to the rescue. The company came up on the double and drove off the Rebels.[70]

Captain Tyler's patrol during the afternoon made a forced reconnaissance. Union pickets on the Chesterville road were driven in. Tyler, on discovering that the Federals held Pontotoc in force, recalled his men and returned to his camp on the Tupelo road.[71]

The action of Smith and his generals on July 12 had immediate repercussions. General Forrest at 9 a.m. learned that Roddey's division had arrived in the Okolona area, following its forced march down from Corinth. With all his troops in hand, Forrest announced to General Lee that he was ready to receive the foe. He ordered Chalmers to send one of his brigades "to the rear, and to let the enemy come on if he would." Chalmers started Rucker's brigade to the rear, while all the wagons and ordnance trains were parked six miles southeast of Pinson's Hill on the Okolona Stage Road. About 6 p.m., as Chalmers was preparing to

68 *O.R.*, Series I, Vol. 39, pt. 1, 304, 308-309, 325.

69 Ibid., 321, 325.

70 Ibid., 301.

71 Ibid., 345.

withdraw the rest of his command, Col. M. C. Galloway of Forrest's staff galloped up on a sweat-lathered horse. He told Chalmers to remain where he was, as Generals Lee and Forrest would be up before morning, "with all the force, to give battle there." Rucker and the wagon trains had already been ordered back.[72]

The reason for this change in plans was Smith's failure, on the 12th, to press on toward Okolona, where the Confederate leaders had planned to fight. Forrest voiced fears that A. J. Smith, because of his pause at Pontotoc, was preparing to call off his expedition and return to Memphis. General Lee likewise was impatient and wished to bring matters to a head. At the moment, his department was being threatened on two other fronts. General Slocum from Vicksburg had recrossed the Big Black, after his return from Jackson, and was beating up the country between the Big Black and Bayou Pierre. It was apparent that Wirt Adams had too few men to cope with Slocum's powerful column. General Maury at Mobile was expecting an amphibious attack at any minute and was calling for reinforcements. Lee promised to send Maury 2,000 to 3,000 men as soon as they had settled matters with A. J. Smith. There had been an understanding between Lee and Forrest that if Smith did not "succeed in delaying the battle," Lee would have "time to wind up his fight" before doing so. Lee, in view of the situation at Mobile and east of the Big Black, was pleased with Forrest's decision to force the issue.[73]

After the decision had been made to accept battle wherever it was offered, and to assail Smith if he "attempted a retreat," Lee directed Forrest "to move everything to the front," while Colonel Galloway was sent on his mission to

72 Ibid., 325; Young, *Seventh Tennessee Cavalry*, 96.

73 *O.R.*, Series I, Vol. 39, pt. 1, 321; *O.R.*, Series 1, Vol. 39, pt. 2, 700, 702; Lee, "Battle of Tupelo," *Publications*, Vol. 6, 43.

Chalmers's command post. Before leaving Okolona, Forrest issued marching orders to his infantry and artillery.[74]

Colonel Bell at the same time was directed by Forrest to return to the front and report to General Chalmers. Leaving Okolona, Bell's Tennesseans rode up the Stage Road. At Prairie Mound, they encountered the 2d Tennessee. Barteau's men and horses were badly jaded, and Bell called for Barteau to halt, feed, rest his men and horses, and to rejoin the brigade in the morning. Bell then pushed on and did not call another halt until reaching Pinson's Hill.[75]

It was well after dark by the time Generals Lee and Forrest reached Pinson's Hill. They were accompanied by the dismounted division and the artillery. General Buford reported to the two senior officers, and cautioned them that up to this moment he "had discovered no evidence of the reported demoralized condition of the enemy, but had found him ever ready for action."[76]

74 *O.R.*, Series I, Vol. 39, pt. 1, 321.

75 Ibid., 325; Hancock, *Diary*, 415. The 2d Tennessee had quit their camp west of Verona early that morning, and had marched southwestward to the Okolona Stage Road, then up that road to within nine miles of Pontotoc. Orders were then received to report to Colonel Bell at Okolona. When within four miles of Okolona, Colonel Barteau encountered Generals Lee and Forrest riding up the Stage Road. He then countermarched his regiment and reported to Colonel Bell at Prairie Mound. The 2d Tennessee rejoined the brigade about daybreak on the 13th.

76 *O.R.*, Series I, Vol. 39, pt. 1, 330. || A native Kentuckian born into considerable wealth, Abraham H. Buford graduated from the Military Academy at West Point in 1841, serving in the First U.S. Dragoons. He saw service on the frontier and in Mexico. Physically, he was very large, "weighing well over three hundred pounds and standing over six feet tall." He commanded an infantry brigade for much of 1863, but returned to cavalry leadership in March, 1864, serving under Forrest. His division was instrumental in routing the Federals at Brice's Crossroads. See Marshall D. Krolick, "Brig. Gen. Abraham H. Buford," in Bruce S. Allardice and Lawrence Lee Hewitt, eds. *Kentuckians in Gray, Confederate Generals and Officers of the Bluegrass State* (Lexington, 2008), 49-55.

3

A. J. SMITH STEALS A MARCH

UNION General A. J. Smith spent the afternoon on July 12, 1864, evaluating the information gathered by Grierson's cavalry. He was impressed by the strength of the Confederate position astride the Okolona Stage Road at Pinson's Hill. The reports brought in by the patrol sent out the Tupelo road, along with information secured by questioning civilians and slaves, led Smith to conclude that the Confederates had concentrated to the southeast of Pontotoc, leaving Tupelo unprotected. After discussing the situation with General Grierson and Colonel Burgh of the 9th Illinois, Smith determined to outflank the Rebel Pinson's Hill line. To keep the Confederates pinned in position, Smith had his cavalry continue, throughout the afternoon, its demonstrations on the Okolona Stage Road. Orders were now issued alerting the division and brigade commanders to have their units ready to resume the march at daybreak on July 13. When they did, they would march on Tupelo, not Okolona.[1]

As his horsesoldiers would have the advance, General Grierson saw that Colonels Winslow and Coon held early reveille. The 3d Iowa of Winslow's brigade would spearhead the march. As Capt. John Brown's battalion was holding the

1 *O.R.*, Series I, Vol. 39, pt. 1, 250-251.

hill on the Houston road, Colonel Noble sent word for it to hold its ground until the army's rear had cleared Pontotoc. This business taken care of, Noble had "Boots and Saddles" sounded. Countermarching, the cavalry division passed through Pontotoc and rode out the Tupelo road.

After an advance of five miles, the Union advance guard encountered Captain Tyler's Kentuckians. Tyler at daybreak had organized another reconnaissance, and, on encountering the 3d Iowa, he had deployed his men across the road, "not knowing whether it was a movement in force or a foraging party." After about 25 minutes of skirmishing, Colonel Noble threw forward a strong force which threatened Tyler's flanks and front. Abandoning the roadblock, the Rebels retired, keeping up a running fight, until they reached the forks of the road, 12 miles east of Pontotoc. Here the Confederates turned into the Verona road, while the bluecoats rode on toward Tupelo.[2]

Smith's infantry and artillery had been turned out and formed, ready to march, at 2:30 a.m. The footsoldiers were kept standing in ranks for a number of hours until all of Grierson's cavalry, except the 7th Kansas and Brown's battalion which were to screen the rear, had cleared the Pontotoc area. When the infantry marched, Colonel Moore's division took the lead followed by General Mower's.[3]

2 Ibid., 304, 306, 309, 345. Brown's Battalion of the 3d Iowa had a narrow escape. Brown and his troopers failed to get the word that Bouton had withdrawn his pickets on the Okolona Stage Road. The first the Iowans knew that this had happened was when they saw Mabry's Mississippians across their line of retreat. Brown formed his battalion in column on the brow of the hill, and, "calling upon every man who could keep his saddle to follow him," charged the foe. Pounding down off the hill, the Federals brushed the surprised Confederates aside and succeeded, after a hard ride, in rejoining the regiment at Tupelo. Ibid., 309.

3 Scott, *Story of the 32d Iowa Infantry*, 291; Cloyd Bryner, *Bugle Echoes, The Story of the Illinois 47th* (Springfield, 1905), 127.

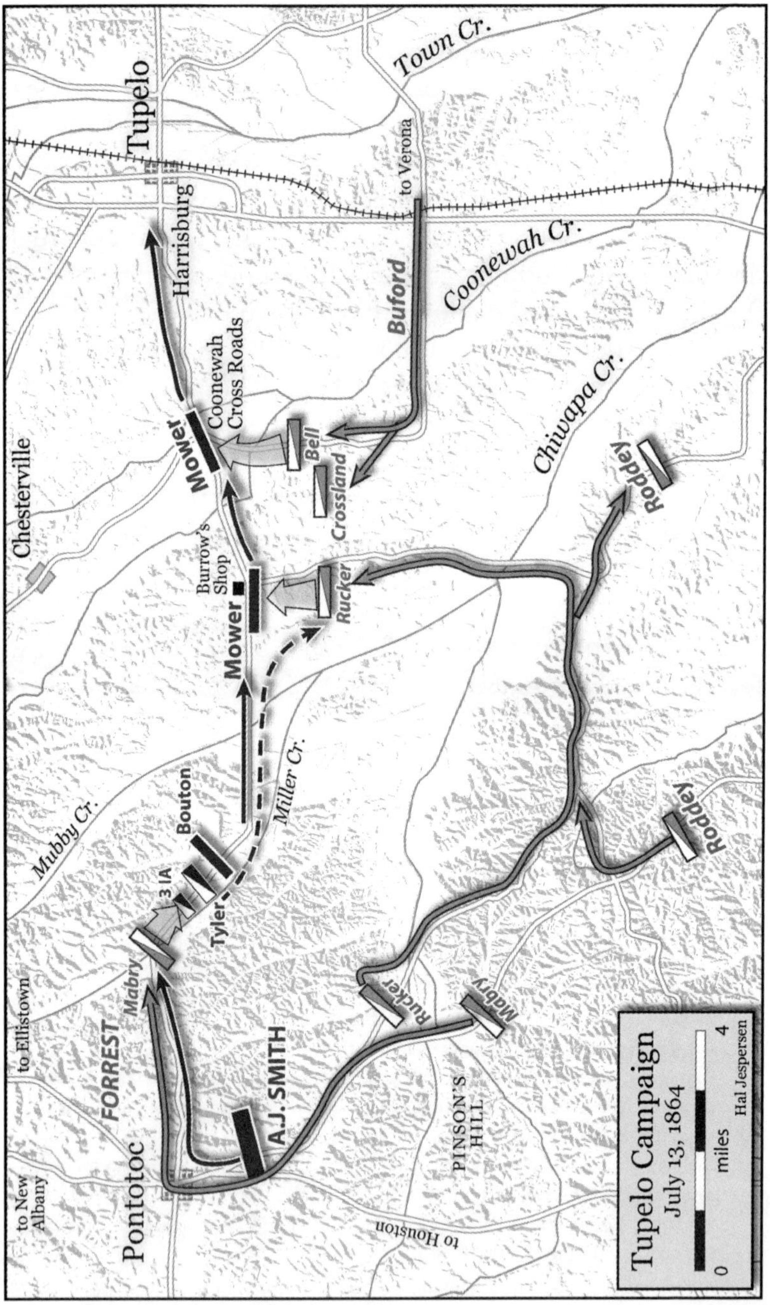
Tupelo Campaign
July 13, 1864
0
4
miles
Hal Jespersen
Tupelo
Town Cr.
to Verona
Harrisburg
Coonewah Cross Roads
Coonewah Cr.
Buford
Chesterville
Mower
Bell
Crossland
Chiwapa Cr.
Roddey
Burrow's Shop
Rucker
Mower
Miller Cr.
Mubby Cr.
Bouton
3 IA
Tyler
Mabry
FORREST
to Ellistown
A.J. SMITH
Rucker
Mabry
Roddey
PINSON'S HILL
Pontotoc
to New Albany
to Houston

On July 13, 1864, as General Forrest prepared to give battle somewhere between Pontotoc and Okolona, Maj. Gen. A. J. Smith abruptly changed direction. Turning east, he marched his Federal infantry to Tupelo and also occupied the small adjoining hamlet of Harrisburg.

Shortly before Moore's division moved out, Colonel Bouton had advanced the 61st U.S. Colored Troops to hold the ridge southeast of Pontotoc vacated by Moore's troops and covering the Okolona Stage Road. By 7 a.m. the soldiers of the 61st sighted a Confederate column coming up the road. Col. F. A. Kendrick deployed and threw forward Company A to establish a roadblock and delay the Rebels. Meanwhile, Colonel Bouton, having learned that Mower's rearguard had left Pontotoc, put the remainder of his brigade and trains in motion. The 7th Kansas Cavalry protected the brigade's rear as it tramped rapidly through Pontotoc and turned into the Tupelo road.[4]

One of Mower's brigades, Col. Lyman Ward's, had been detailed to guard the flanks of "the wagon train, the white canvas covers having always great attraction for Forrest's followers." To accomplish this mission, Ward divided his command into 25-man detachments, and distributed these along the right flank of the train—a detachment to each six wagons.[5]

Smith, whose object was to secure a lodgment on the Mobile & Ohio Railroad as well as to choose ground and await an attack, had issued orders for the units to keep well closed up and not halt unless absolutely necessary.[6]

The confusion caused by the sudden change in Confederate battle plans on the night of July 12 aided the Federals' movement of the 13th. The withdrawal of Rucker's

4 *O.R.*, Series I, Vol. 39, pt. 1, 276, 301.

5 Ibid., 276; Bryner, *Bugle Echoes*, 127.

6 Bryner, *Bugle Echoes*, 127.

brigade and the 2d Tennessee had left the Pontotoc-Tupelo road unguarded at a critical period. His brigade was back on the Cotton Gin road by daybreak, but Rucker did not feel authorized to act upon his old orders—to watch the Tupelo road. Though his scouts sighted a strong Union column marching eastward from Pontotoc, Rucker, after notifying Chalmers of this development, took no steps to delay the Union advance. Instead of marching to Tyler's support, Chalmers and Rucker anxiously awaited orders from Forrest. This lack of initiative on their part was to cost the Confederates dearly. Grierson's division had covered half the 18 miles separating Pontotoc and Tupelo before any orders from Forrest were received.[7]

Several hours before, Colonel Mabry, whose brigade during the night had taken position in front of Pinson's Hill, discovered and reported to General Buford at 6 a.m. that the Yankees to his front were pulling back. Mabry and his men cautiously advanced. Before they had gone very far, Generals Lee and Forrest rode up, accompanied by Forrest's escort and the Pettus Flying Artillery. The advance was pressed to within a short distance of Pontotoc, where the 61st U.S.C.T. was encountered. As the Negroes retired through the town and out the Tupelo road, Generals Lee and Forrest realized that A. J. Smith had stolen a march on them and was striking rapidly eastward for Tupelo.

After a hurried discussion of the situation, Lee told Forrest to take Mabry's brigade, Forrest's Alabama Cavalry Regiment, the escort company, and the Pettus Flying Artillery and to harass the foe's rear. Lee would ride with Chalmers' and Buford's divisions and endeavor to cross over from the Okolona Stage Road and assail Smith's right "at every vulnerable point."[8]

7 *O.R.*, Series I, Vol. 39, pt. 1, 325-326.

8 Ibid., 321, 330, 336, 339, 346, 349; Lee, "Battle of Tupelo," *Publications*, Vol. 6, 43; Hancock, *Diary*, 416.

Lee promptly contacted General Buford and told him to march for Verona, via the Pontotoc-Camargo Ferry road. This would place Buford's people on the Yankees' right. As they swung into the saddle, Bell's brigade took the lead, followed by the Kentucky Brigade. Before he had traveled very far, Buford was directed by Lee to make an administrative change. General Lyon was relieved from his brigade and ordered to assume command of the division of dismounted infantry. Col. Edward Crossland, as senior officer present, took over the Kentucky Brigade.[9] Several critical hours were to pass, however, before Lee was able to contact General Chalmers. Chalmers, after learning from Rucker that the Federals were en route for Tupelo, had assumed that Lee and Forrest had again changed their plan and would fight the Federals on the approaches to Okolona. Fearful that the Federals, having stolen a march on the Confederates, would get there first, Chalmers called up Roddey's division and Rucker's brigade and set out for the Chiwapa fords. He was determined to hold these crossings long enough to permit Lee and Forrest to complete their dispositions to receive an attack.[10]

Forrest lost no time in carrying out his part of the plan. Colonel Mabry was told to force his way into Pontotoc.[11] Attacking with their characteristic abandon, Mabry's Mississippians, supported by Forrest's Regiment and the escort company, brushed aside the 7th Kansas Cavalry and Company A, 61st U.S. Colored Troops. As his horsesoldiers retreated through the town, Col. Thomas P. Herrick of the 7th Kansas sent a call for help to Colonel Bouton, whose rearguard was several miles east of Pontotoc. Shouting to Colonel Kendrick of the 61st, Bouton told him to ambush

9 *O.R.*, Series I, Vol. 39, pt. 1, 321, 330, 339, 346, 349.

10 Ibid., 325-326.

11 Before Lee and Forrest parted, Col. Isham Harrison rode up with his 6th Mississippi Cavalry and reported to Colonel Mabry.

the onrushing Rebels. Two companies of blacks were double-timed into the underbrush flanking the road. There they waited until the 7th Kansas and the panting soldiers of Company A had passed, and as Mabry's vanguard thundered to within 12 paces, they cut loose a well-aimed volley which emptied a score of saddles and threw the pursuing column into confusion. Skillfully disengaging his men, Kendrick retired a mile down the road and prepared another ambush. This time it was not so successful. The pursuit continued.

About five miles from Pontotoc, as the rear of Bouton's column descended a grade and crossed Miller Creek, Mabry came on hard. To support the Mississippians, General Forrest brought up a section of guns manned by the Pettus Flying Artillery. Throwing their two 10-pounder Parrotts into battery, the butternuts shelled the "column furiously," but did little damage. Bouton's troops hurried onward until they gained the opposite ridge, where the redlegs of Battery I, 2d U.S. Colored Artillery, unlimbered their guns and returned the fire of the Rebels at a range of 800 yards. The 59th U.S. Colored Troops was deployed to the left of the battery, the 61st U.S.C.T. to the right of the road, while the 68th U.S.C.T. was held in reserve. The sight of the Union battle line made the Confederates cautious, and they took a long time in deploying. Meanwhile, the wagon train, guarded by Ward's brigade, was rolling eastward and had crossed Mubby Creek. Bouton, seeing that quite an interval now separated his brigade from the train, sent the 68th U.S.C.T. to close the gap. It was soon followed by the 61st U.S.C.T. and a section of the battery. Maj. James C. Foster of the 59th U.S.C.T. now deployed his troops in support of the remaining section of Battery I. Two companies were deployed to the left, three to the right, and a battalion held in reserve. Just as the reserve was taking cover in a thicket, Major Foster saw a cloud of dust coming toward him. The cannoneers of Battery I opened fire.

Forrest's Regiment and the escort company, having forded Miller Creek, beat their way across a cornfield and advanced against the 59th's left flank. Foster hurried up one company from the reserve, and the Negroes waited until the greyclads were within 15 yards before they blazed away. After a brief fire-fight, the Confederates pulled back. As Bouton and his officers were exchanging mutual congratulations, they sighted a strong Confederate column, Mabry's Mississippians, bearing down on their right flank. An orderly was sent galloping to alert General Mower to this threat to the rearguard.[12]

The two cannon were now withdrawn, and Major Foster was ordered to retire with his regiment, leaving a strong skirmish line to protect the rear. Two companies, B and H, were deployed as skirmishers, and the regiment, after beating off an attack by Mabry's vanguard, retreated and rejoined the brigade.[13]

About a mile east of Mubby Creek, Bouton again faced his brigade about and formed it into line of battle. This time the Confederates did not attack, as General Forrest, taking cognizance that no attack had yet been made on the right flank of the Union column, voiced fears that he was driving the foe too rapidly. He therefore halted his command to wait for Lee to strike.[14]

Not being pressed, Bouton recalled his regiments and sent forward all his brigade, except seven companies of the 61st U.S.C.T. Meanwhile, General Mower, acting upon Bouton's call for help, had directed Colonel Ward to recall the 33d Wisconsin from duty as flankers and post it in rear of the train. This move uncovered about one-fourth

12 Ibid., 301-302, 321, 349; Cowden, *History of the 59th U.S.C.T.*, 127-128. Two companies from the reserve were called up by Major Foster to support the right.

13 Cowden, *History of the 59th U.S.C.T.*, 128-129.

14 *O.R.*, Series I, Vol. 39, pt. 1, 301, 302, 321.

BRIG. GEN.
JAMES R. CHALMERS

A Mississippi lawyer in peacetime, Chalmers commanded Forrest's First Cavalry Division.

Library of Congress

the wagons. All the while the long column continued to push ahead, as Bouton's people confronted Forrest. About 2 p.m. the train began passing Burrow's Shop, eight miles east of Tupelo, where a side road intersected the Tupelo road. Here the flankers of the 14th Wisconsin were furiously assailed.[15]

This slashing attack was spearheaded by the 8th Mississippi Cavalry of Rucker's brigade. While en route to hold the Chiwapa fords, Chalmers had been overtaken by one of General Lee's aides, who directed him to push for the Pontotoc-Tupelo road and "to attack the enemy vigorously in the flank." After telling Roddey to continue the march to the Chiwapa, Chalmers turned Rucker's brigade into the road that intersected the Tupelo road at Burrow's Shop. The brigade encountered some difficulty in crossing Chiwapa Creek, while the road leading to Burrow's shop, which followed a ridge, was narrow. Rucker's march was accordingly slowed, and much of the train had passed the strategic intersection before Rucker's lead regiment, the 8th Mississippi, pounded into view. Attacking immediately, the hell-for-leather Mississippians broke through the 14th Wisconsin, reached the wagons, and began shooting the mules. Lt. Col. James W. Polleys of the Wisconsin regiment

15 Ibid., 276, 302.

failed to panic. Rallying his men, he posted them parallel with the train facing from the road. Colonel Ward brought up the 33d Wisconsin on the double and stationed it behind a rail fence, running at a right angle to the road. From the fence, they opened a murderous fire on the left flank of Rucker's people as they assailed the 14th Wisconsin. Ward, seeing that the Confederates were badly shaken by the crashing volleys of the 33d, bellowed for Polleys's soldiers to charge. The bluecoats stormed ahead, scattering Rucker's horsesoldiers. In their haste to get away, the Confederates left their dead and seriously wounded on the field, along with the colors of the 8th Mississippi Cavalry.

Ward, on inspecting the train, saw a number of dead mules, shot in their traces. Time being of the essence, Ward had the dead animals cut loose from their harnesses, while seven wagons damaged by the carelessness of the teamsters were pushed aside. After they had been unloaded and the wheels removed, they were set afire.[16]

Colonel Bouton had watched as Rucker's column drove down on the wagon train. He also observed that Forrest's people were again threatening to envelop his rearguard. The brigade adjutant galloped ahead to warn Mower that the train was about to be assailed. While Ward's people were recovering the wagons, Bouton continued to fight a delaying

16 Ibid., 251, 257, 276-277, 326; Young, *Seventh Tennessee Cavalry*, 96-97; Lee, "The Battle of Tupelo," *Publications*, Vol. 6, 43; Hancock, *Diary*, 416-417. Maj. C. C. Clay of the 7th Tennessee Cavalry was wounded in the fight at Burrow's Shop. Chalmers reported that in addition to the seven wagons, the Federals abandoned one caisson and two ambulances. | | James R. Chalmers was a Mississippi lawyer and colonel of the 9th Mississippi Infantry. Promoted to a brigadier's rank in February, 1862, he demonstrated conspicuous courage at Shiloh, and was wounded at Stones River. Transferred back to Mississippi in 1863, he served thereafter with cavalry. When Forrest was similarly transferred back to Mississippi in November, 1863, Chalmers and his cavalry were placed in Forrest's corps. He served Forrest well, proving to be as aggressive and able a cavalryman as he was an infantry brigadier. Terry Jones, "James Ronald Chalmers," in *The Confederate General*, I: 168-171.

action. In protecting the army's rear as it marched slowly eastward, Bouton continued to employ the 59th and 61st U.S. Colored Troops, while holding the recently recruited 68th U.S.C.T. in reserve. Forrest on reaching Burrow's Shop joined forces with Chalmers. With two brigades (Rucker's and Mabry's) reinforced by Forrest's Alabama Cavalry Regiment, the escort company, and the Pettus Flying Artillery, Forrest continued to harass Bouton.[17]

After the withdrawal of Tyler's combat patrol from their front, the march of Grierson's cavalry toward Tupelo was uninterrupted. Grierson halted his division about noon to allow the men to feed their mounts, while Maj. Martin H. Williams with his regiment, the 10th Missouri Cavalry, and two companies of the 3d Iowa thundered into Tupelo. They were followed soon after by the rest of the division. Colonels Winslow and Coon, in accordance with instructions from Grierson, employed units from their brigades to picket the roads leading into Tupelo and to wreck the railroad. Battalions from the 4th Iowa and the 9th Illinois advanced down the Mobile & Ohio beyond Stanislaus Depot ripping up track and burning trestles.[18]

General A. J. Smith refused to allow the attacks on his rearguard to turn him aside from his three-fold goal of securing Tupelo, gaining a lodgment on the Mobile & Ohio, and selecting ground of his choosing on which to accept battle. He called for "the column to keep well closed up and move steadily forward without halting, unless absolutely necessary."[19] To comply with these instructions, General Mower, as soon as Ward's infantrymen had repulsed Rucker, started the column on. This time, however, his division

17 *O.R.*, Series I, Vol. 39, pt. 1, 302, 321, 326; Cowden, *History of the 59th U.S.C.T.*, 129.

18 *O.R.*, Series I, Vol. 39, pt. 1, 304, 306, 309, 314, 316,317; Scott, *Story of a Cavalry Regiment*, 286-287; *History of the 9th Illinois Cavalry*, 120.

19 *O.R.*, Series I, Vol. 39, pt. 1, 251.

would march behind the train. Scouts soon reported another Confederate column coming up rapidly from the southeast. The newcomers belonged to Buford's division. Acting under orders from General Lee, Buford had ridden to intercept the Yankees at the head of Bell's brigade and a section of Morton's Tennessee Battery. Buford at Verona had turned his column into the Birmingham road, which led northward and intersected the Pontotoc-Tupelo road at Coonewah Crossroads, five miles west of Tupelo.

As he approached Coonewah Creek, Buford sighted Smith's army as it marched eastward. Buford, turning to Colonel Bell, told him to dismount his brigade, cross the creek, and assail the Yankees. Every fifth man was detailed as a horse-holder, and the Rebels forded the creek, and prepared to push on toward the train, one-half mile to their front. The 2d Tennessee was first to wade Coonewah Creek, and Buford, before the rest of the brigade had crossed, had Colonel Barteau deploy his men parallel to the road, along which the bluecoats were marching. So certain was Buford of capturing at least part of the wagons that he called out as the 2d Tennessee moved out, "Boys, do not kill the mules, but turn them down this way."

Because of Buford's impatience, the 2d Tennessee was beating its way through the underbrush toward the train, before the other regiments were ready to take up the advance. The 15th Tennessee, coming up on the double, filed into position on the left of the 2d Tennessee. Fighting had commenced before the 16th Tennessee and Newsom's Regiment were formed. Buford was about to be taught a lesson he should have learned at the Military Academy: an attack made before all one's units were in position is certain to be smashed.[20]

20 Ibid., 330, 347; Hancock, *Diary*, 417.

Because of the dense undergrowth between the road and Coonewah Creek, the Federals (McMillan's brigade) against whom Bell's people advanced were taken by surprise. Mower's division, which was guarding the train, marched as follows: Col. William L. McMillen's brigade in the lead, next Col. Alexander Wilkin's, then Col. Joseph J. Woods's, with Colonel Ward's bringing up the rear. It was fortunate for the Federals that Buford had opened the engagement before all of Bell's people had been deployed. McMillen quickly rallied his men—the 72d and the 95th Ohio were formed on the double in a field south of the road, while the cannoneers of the 2d Iowa Battery and Lt. Orrin W. Cram's section of Battery E, 1st Illinois Light Artillery, unlimbered their guns. Seeing that the Tennesseans had closed to within a few rods of the Iowans' guns, the 114th Illinois rushed to their support. One of Cram's guns was put out of action by the fall of one of the wheel-horses, while one of the caissons was upset and its team decimated.[21]

General Mower was riding with Colonel Wilkin, and he ordered the pace quickened. As soldiers of the 2d Brigade hurried forward, they passed a number of McMillen's men who had panicked and walking wounded. Sighting the 2d Iowa Battery "playing upon the Rebels as rapidly as their guns could be loaded," Wilkin sent the 9th Minnesota into the woods on the right of the 114th Illinois. Before the Minnesotans could take position 50 rods south of the road, they saw a number of men dressed in blue beating their way toward the gap separating the two brigades. Wilkin, seeing that the newcomers were pointing their rifle-muskets at the 2d Iowa Battery, shouted for the 9th to fire. A volley scattered the onrushing Tennesseans. The 47th Illinois now

21 *O.R.*, Series I, Vol. 39, pt. 1, 259, 261, 278, 330, 347. The 93d Illinois of McMillen's brigade had been detached earlier in the day and sent forward as an escort to Moore's train, while the 10th Minnesota had passed beyond the point assailed by the Confederates. Ibid., 262, 264.

dashed up and filed into position on the right of the 9th Minnesota, and together they pressed the Confederates to their front. The detachment of the 5th Minnesota and 8th Wisconsin was sent to support the 2d Iowa Battery, while the 11th Missouri was held in reserve.[22]

Colonel Woods, when the firing commenced to his front, saw that his lead regiment, the 35th Iowa, was formed into line of battle south of the road with skirmishers advanced. Confederate sharpshooters who had infiltrated the underbrush north of Coonewah Creek and had been sniping at Wilkin's train fled. Moments later, dismounted troopers of the 15th Tennessee opened a heavy fire on the right flank of the 7th Minnesota and 12th Iowa as they tramped along beside the wagons. Two flankers from Company D, 12th Iowa, were captured. The underbrush, south of the road at this point, was so thick that the Iowans had trouble deploying and taking cover in a shallow ravine. Opposite the area where the 7th Minnesota formed was an old field that had been allowed to grow up in weeds. While the Minnesotans charged across the field, the Iowans crouched and allowed the Tennesseans to close to within 20 paces before they fired. Woods's people more than held their own in a fight with the 15th Tennessee.[23]

Buford had botched the attack on the train at Coonewah Crossroads. By the time Newsom's Regiment and the 16th Tennessee had forded Coonewah Creek and advanced to the assistance of the 2d and 15th Tennessee, the Yankees had recovered from the surprise. The 2d Tennessee finding itself overlapped on both flanks broke. Colonel Barteau rallied his men on the brigade. Bell's people struggled to hold their position pending the arrival of the Kentucky Brigade.

22 Ibid., 265, 267; Bryner, *Bugle Echoes*, 128.

23 *O.R.*, Series I, Vol. 39, pt. 1, 268, 270, 271, 272, 274, 347; Reed, *12th Iowa*, 152. Woods's other regiment, the 33d Missouri, remained with the wagons as they rolled eastward.

But the ease with which the Federals were able to throw in reserves tipped the scales. Having suffered heavy losses in the fight, Bell's Tennesseans fled across Coonewah Creek. There they were rallied on the horse-holders.[24]

Colonel Crossland, at the head of the Kentucky Brigade, reached Coonewah Creek after Bell's brigade had recrossed. Crossland, in accordance with instructions from Buford, dismounted his men and formed them into line to cover Bell's retreat. As soon as Bell had re-formed his brigade, Buford had the men remount.[25]

In view of General Smith's desire to occupy a strong position in and around Tupelo and to await attack, General Mower had his brigade commanders recall their troops as soon as the Rebels disappeared from their front. After the dead and wounded had been collected, the march was resumed.

Forrest had continued to harass the Union rearguard. The long afternoon was now drawing to a close and dusk was at hand. Colonel Bouton saw that the day had sapped the vigor of the 59th and 61st U.S. Colored Troops, and as the brigade passed Coonewah Crossroads, he was compelled to commit the 68th U.S.C.T. Four companies were deployed in the timber and told to hold their fire until the Rebels "were close on them." Mabry's vanguard soon pounded into view. Meanwhile, dismounted troopers of the 12th Kentucky of Crossland's brigade had forded Coonewah Creek. Assailed from two directions, the battalion of the 68th U.S.C.T. gave way.[26]

24 *O.R.*, Series I, Vol. 39, pt. 1, 330, 347; Hancock, *Diary*, 417-418. Colonel Bell reported that in this engagement, which continued but a few minutes, his loss "was very heavy." Colonel Barteau listed casualties in his 2d Tennessee, as 30 or more killed or wounded, including six officers badly wounded.

25 *O.R.*, Series I, Vol. 39, pt. 1, 330, 336, 339, 341, 342.

26 Ibid., 302, 321-322, 342.

The Federals, after passing Coonewah Crossroads, were subjected to no more attacks, beyond an occasional projectile from one of Morton's guns. One of the Rebel guns, from a masked position south of Coonewah Creek, shelled a section of the Tupelo road. Mower and several of his officers voiced fears that the teamsters might panic, so the veterans tried to display an outward calm as they marched steadily ahead. When the 12th Iowa crossed the beaten zone, Chaplain Frederick Humphrey, who had joined the regiment a few days before, galloped to the head of the column and looked squarely into the faces of Lt. Col. John H. Stibbs and Adjutant Nathaniel Duncan. When asked what was wanted, he replied, "I wanted to look into your faces to see if I could discover how veterans feel in battle, and I want to know, Colonel, what my duties are in a case like this."

He was told that he might report to the surgeon and be ready to assist the wounded. Just then two artillerists were knocked from their caisson, wounded. "Would it be right for me to assist these men?" he inquired. When told that it was, he dismounted and assisted in loading the wounded into an ambulance.[27]

General Smith, on learning that Grierson's cavalry had possession of Tupelo, issued orders for the trains, as they came up, to be parked about two miles west of the railroad. Colonel Moore was directed to form his division south of the Pontotoc road, facing west. Here he would be in position to cover Mower's division and Bouton's brigade as they came in. Grierson was told to rush some of his cavalry out the Pontotoc road to relieve Bouton's people, who were hard-pressed by the Rebels.

Three battalions of cavalry (two from the 9th Illinois and one from the 4th Iowa) rode westward to assist Bouton. The Negroes and their white officers were glad to see the

27 Reed, *12th Iowa*, 153-154.

horsesoldiers. Screened by the cavalry, Bouton's brigade tramped on and at 9 o'clock went into camp in an open field near the supply train. Forrest by this time had called up a four-gun battery which shelled the bluecoats, but beyond causing the men to duck for cover did little damage.[28]

Colonel Moore, as directed, halted and formed his division into battle line on the high ground overlooking Harrisburg Branch, two miles west of Tupelo. Col. Charles D. Murray's brigade was posted on the right, its right flank anchored on the Pontotoc road.[29] Col. Edward H. Wolfe's brigade was posted on Murray's left, except for the 117th Illinois which occupied a commanding ridge on the division's left.[30] Col. James I. Gilbert's brigade was encamped to the rear and on the left flank of the wagon corral, with the mission of guarding the train.[31]

Mower's division crossed Harrisburg Branch at 8 p.m. and prepared to camp north of the Pontotoc road, while the wagons were corralled south of the road on the high ground overlooking Kings Creek. Bouton's black brigade bivouacked for the night near the train.[32]

Grierson's horsesoldiers, except those assigned picket duty, spent the night of July 13 in Tupelo.[33]

General Buford, accompanied by Bell's and Crossland's brigades, reported to General Forrest on the evening of the

28 *O.R.*, Series I, Vol. 39, pt. 1, 302, 306, 312, 317, 322; Cowden, *History of the 59th U.S.C.T.*, 129. The 2d and 3d Battalions of the 4th Iowa and a battalion of the 9th Illinois were absent wreaking havoc on the railroad south of Tupelo.

29 *O.R.*, Series I, Vol. 39, pt. 1, 279-280, 282. From right to left the regiments were posted: the 122d Illinois, the 89th Indiana, the 58th Illinois, the 21st Missouri, and the 119th Illinois. Murray's line was perpendicular with the road.

30 Ibid., 295.

31 Ibid., 280; Scott, *Story of the 32d Iowa*, 291.

32 *O.R.*, Series I, Vol. 39, pt. 1, 251; Cowden, *History of the 59th U.S.C.T.*, 129.

33 *O.R.*, Series I, Vol. 39, pt. 1, 304, 306, 309, 312, 314, 316, 137. The 3d Iowa Cavalry camped on Younger's plantation. One battalion of the 9th Illinois picketed the Okolona road and the 3d Iowa watched the road to Ellistown.

13th at Coonewah Crossroads. Chalmers joined Forrest at the camp formerly occupied by the dismounted cavalry, four miles west of Tupelo. The day had been excessively hot and the dismounted cavalry under General Lyon had lagged. Darkness had closed in by the time Forrest had his corps in hand. From his scouts he learned that the foe had halted somewhere between Harrisburg and Tupelo. Anxious to learn the exact position of the foe, Forrest moved Mabry's brigade forward and had the gunners of the Pettus Flying Artillery hurl several rounds into the bluecoats' encampment. When there was no reply, Forrest called on Buford to relieve Mabry's brigade, which had been in the saddle for 24 hours, with the Kentucky Brigade. Crossland brought his people forward and established and manned a picket line within two miles of Harrisburg. The other Confederate brigades camped for the night.[34]

If General Smith and his officers congratulated themselves on the evening of July 13, 1864, they could be excused. The day had gone extremely well for them. They had stolen a march on the dreaded Forrest and had occupied a strong position of their choosing. If the Confederates assaulted them here, they were confident that they could defeat them. In the day's fighting, the Union infantry had more than held its own in the face of slashing attacks by Forrest's mounted infantry. Colonel Bouton's brigade of Negroes had acquitted themselves with honor at the expense of Mabry's brigade, with which Forrest rode. Rucker's effort to destroy the train and sever the column at Burrow's Shop and Bell's attack designed to achieve a similar goal at Coonewah Crossroads had been repulsed by Mower's footsoldiers.

34 Ibid., 322, 326, 330, 336, 349; Hancock, *Diary*, 418; Lee, "Battle of Tupelo," *Publications*, Vol. 6, 43. The 2d Tennessee was assigned to picket the Verona-Pontotoc road.

4

SMITH'S TROOPS MAUL FORREST'S CORPS

ALTHOUGH their energy had been sapped by "the heavy work and intense heat of the day," Generals Lee and Forrest dismounted, and, moving beyond hearing distance of their staffs, they discussed the situation. Undoubtedly, the two generals were keenly disappointed with the day's results. Lee was seated on the ground, his back against a tree, while Forrest in his shirt-sleeves, having doffed his coat and spread it on the ground, was lying down at full length. Suddenly, Forrest scrambled to his feet, put on his coat, mounted his horse, and shouted for Lt. Samuel Donelson of his staff to come with him, as he had determined to make a personal reconnaissance of the foe's position.

Riding through the woods and fields, the two officers made a wide swing and came up well in rear of Smith's army. They soon found themselves among the wagons, where teamsters were foraging their animals. About one-half hour after they had started, Forrest said to Donelson, "I have left my pistols." Donelson answered that he had one, and offered it to the general, who declined, saying, "It doesn't matter much anyway. I don't think we will have any use for them." It was too dark for the Federals to distinguish the color of their uniforms, and little notice was taken of the two horsemen as they passed to the rear of the encampment.

Forrest, having satisfied himself as to the position of the foe, turned in the direction of his command post. They had gone about 200 yards when they were challenged by two bluecoated pickets. Riding up to them, Forrest, in an indignant tone, inquired, "What do you mean by halting your commanding officer?" and without another remark passed the sentries. Too late they realized that they had been fooled, and they called for the riders to halt. Anticipating that they would be fired upon, Forrest and Donelson crouched low over their saddles, put the spurs to their mounts, and galloped away. The pickets fired, but they aimed too high, and the two riders escaped.[1]

The Confederates had been roused, fed, and mustered by 2 a.m. on July 14, 1864. Lyon's dismounted division had finally arrived, but the previous day's heat and hard march had taken a heavy toll. Many of the men had straggled. It was daylight before the order to move out was passed. In accordance with instructions from General Buford, the troopers of Mabry's and Bell's brigades swung into their saddles and rode to the crossroads, about a mile and one-half west of Harrisburg, where they found Crossland's Kentuckians manning the picket line. There they were halted, dismounted, and every fifth man detailed as a

1 Wyeth, *Life of General N. B. Forrest*, 439-440. || Parson disputes much of this tale, especially the more sensationalistic elements. Though Forrest and Donelson did make a reconnaissance, the details Donelson described—riding through the enemy wagons, being challenged, Forrest's bluff to the pickets—do not appear in the written record until 1907, well after Forrest and most other potential witnesses to this feat were long dead. Donelson claimed "Forrest laughed and bragged about" this exploit, but it does not appear in either Forrest's own reports or Jordan and Pryor's history of Forrest's Cavalry. Finally, if Donelson's account were true, Forrest's subsequent failure to inform General Lee of those details or adjust Confederate deployments for the next day's attack would amount to gross incompetence. See Parson, *Work for Giants*, 163-166.

COL. EDWARD WINSLOW

Winslow, of the 4th Iowa Cavalry, commanded one of Grierson's mounted brigades.

William F. Scott, *The Story of a Cavalry Regiment, 1893*

horse-holder.[2] Chalmers's division left its horses at the dismounted cavalry's camp and marched to the area where Forrest was marshaling his corps. By the time Chalmers reached the crossroads, Crossland's skirmishers were advancing to engage Union pickets posted north and south of the Pontotoc road.[3]

Daybreak on Thursday, July 14, found Union cavalry picketing the roads leading to General Smith's camps. A battalion of the 3d Iowa and one from the 4th Iowa watched the Pontotoc road, west of Harrisburg. Capt. Benjamin F. Crail was in charge of these outposts.[4] Before sun-up Colonel Winslow called on the remainder of his brigade to undertake a forced reconnaissance of the Pontotoc road. At the picket line, Winslow halted, while he deployed the 10th Missouri Cavalry to the right of the road and the rest of his horsesoldiers to the left. Winslow, after telling Crail and his pickets to hold their ground, waved his

2 *O.R.*, Series I, Vol. 39, pt. 1, 330, 336; Hancock, *Diary*, 421-422. The 2d Tennessee, having been recalled from picket duty, rejoined Bell's brigade about sunrise at Calhoun's Crossroads. A road from Verona intersected the Pontotoc road, a mile and one-half west of Harrisburg.

3 *O.R.*, Series I, Vol. 39, pt. 1, 326.

4 Ibid., 309. Companies E, F, and H, 3d Iowa Cavalry, and four companies of the 4th Iowa, including Companies L and M, reported to Captain Crail.

BRIG. GEN. JOSEPH A. MOWER AND STAFF

The highly capable Mower (center, seated) was Smith's ranking subordinate. Sherman once called him "The boldest man we have."

Library of Congress

men forward. The brigade cautiously felt its way ahead and soon established contact with pickets of Crossland's Kentucky Brigade, covering the Confederate deployment. At first, the bluecoats, as many of them were armed with Spencer carbines, were able to gain ground. North of the Pontotoc road, the 10th Missouri reached the Birmingham road. Here it was halted by Winslow, as he saw that the Rebel leaders were bringing up reinforcements in such numbers as to presage an attack on General Smith's camp. Winslow sent an aide galloping to alert Smith and Grierson to the danger.[5]

General A. J. Smith, on receipt of this warning, had the "long roll" beaten and began forming his soldiers to meet the anticipated attack. The horseman was told to rejoin

5 Ibid., 312, 314, 336, 340, 342; Scott, *Story of a Cavalry Regiment*, 287.

Winslow, tell him to hold his ground until the Rebels had completed their deployment, and then retire within the infantry lines.[6]

As the infantry brigades were falling out, A. J. Smith pointed out to his ranking subordinate, General Mower, the ground north of the Pontotoc road the First Division was to defend. Mower called his four brigade commanders together and gave them their assignments: Col. Joseph J. Woods's 3d Brigade would hold the left, Col. Lyman M. Ward's 4th Brigade the center; Col. William L. McMillen's 1st brigade the right, and Col. Alexander Wilkin's 2d Brigade would constitute the division's ready reserve.[7]

Colonel Woods posted the 12th Iowa on the left. The Iowans were formed in a wooded grove, north of the Pontotoc road, with open fields to their front. The right, Company B, was thrown back at a right angle to connect with the 33d Missouri. Colonel Stibbs had his people throw down the heavy rail fence, behind which they had formed, and pile the rails for protection against small-arms fire. The 7th Minnesota, except two companies (Banks's and Hoag's) was posted in support of the 12th Iowa. To screen his men, Col. William R. Marshall saw that they were sheltered in the edge of a woods west of their camp. Capt. G. T. Banks's and Lt. Loel B. Hoag's companies were advanced and took position between the 12th Iowa and the Pontotoc road. In the forthcoming battle they would look to Colonel Stibbs of the 12th Iowa for orders. Lt. Col. William H. Heath posted his 33d Missouri to the right and at a right angle to the 12th Iowa. The men were told to lie down. Col. Sylvester Hill deployed his 35th Iowa on the right of the 33d Missouri. Both the 33d Missouri

6 *O.R.*, Series I, Vol. 39, pt. 1, 309, 314; Scott, *Story of a Cavalry Regiment*, 287.

7 *O.R.*, Series I, Vol. 39, pt. 1, 257.

and the 35th Iowa faced north, with their backs to the Pontotoc road.[8]

Colonel Ward's bluecoats hurried into position on the right of the 3d Brigade. The 33d Wisconsin was stationed on the crest of a hill, its left resting near a log house on the Pontotoc road, and fronting to the northwest. Colonel Polleys's 14th Wisconsin and a detachment of the 41st Illinois were in reserve, a few paces in rear of the 33d Wisconsin. The cannoneers of the 2d Battery, Iowa Light Artillery, unlimbered their four guns in the interval between Ward's and Woods's brigades, sighting them to command the Pontotoc road and the open fields north of Harrisburg. Capt. Michael Muller of the 6th Battery, Indiana Light Artillery, had his redlegs unlimber their four 3-inch Rodman rifles on the right of Ward's battle line.[9]

Colonel McMillen's 1st Brigade occupied ground on the right of the 6th Indiana Battery. His line of battle was arc-like and faced north and northeast, with its right flank anchored on the Pontotoc road. Each regiment in the brigade detached and advanced one company as skirmishers. Two guns of Battery B, 1st Illinois Light Artillery, were positioned on the right of McMillen's brigade and sighted to command Kings Creek.[10]

Colonel Wilkin's 2d Brigade, as it was to constitute the division reserve, was formed in double line of battle immediately behind Ward's unit. Here Wilkin's people

8 Ibid., 268, 270, 271, 272, 274j Reed, *12th Iowa*, 154. Reed wrote that the 33d Missouri faced northwest and the 35th Iowa was in reserve, while the commanding officers indicated in their "After Action Reports" that their positions were as described. As Reed published his regimental history, 39 years after the event, we question how much he recalled about the positions held by the 33d Missouri and 35th Iowa.

9 *O.R.*, Series I, Vol. 39, pt. 1, 259, 277.

10 Ibid.

were in defilade and would be sheltered from the foe's fire until their presence at the front was required.[11]

At the first sound of firing on the picket line, Colonel Moore had ordered his 1st and 3d brigade commanders to cover their fronts with skirmishers. When Woods's people took position north of the Pontotoc road, it was on ground well in advance of where Moore's 1st Brigade, Murray's, had spent the night. Colonel Murray now brought his brigade forward and aligned it on Woods's left, the regiments "preserving the same order in line."[12] The gunners of the 3d Battery, Indiana Light Artillery, unlimbered three guns on a knoll, with the 122d Illinois on their right and the 89th Indiana on their left. Lt. Richard Burns of the Indiana battery positioned one gun, a 6-pounder James Rifle, to sweep the area in front of Murray's left, and the two 12-pounder Napoleons to cover the field to the front and right. The battery's fourth gun, a 6-pounder James Rifle, under Lt. Philip McPherson was unlimbered on the Pontotoc road in the interval between Woods's left and Murray's right. Colonel Murray saw that his infantry was posted so it would be concealed by the configuration of the terrain from the Rebels' view. His right flank regiment, the 122d Illinois, crouched behind a rail fence at the edge of a cornfield, while the other units were screened by brush.[13]

Colonel Wolfe's 3d Brigade took position on the commanding ridge to the left of Murray's people. The

11 Ibid., 265; Bryner, *Bugle Echoes*, 131-132. | | Col. Alexander Wilkin was, in historian Thomas Parson's words, "an outstanding soldier." He was "a Yale lawyer," served in the Mexican-American War, and in this conflict had already seen "combat at Bull Run, Mill Springs, and Corinth. He was also one of the few officers to come out of the Brice's Crossroads fight with both his brigade and his reputation intact." Parson, *Work for Giants*, 159.

12 *O.R.*, Series I, Vol. 39, pt. 1, 280, 282. From right to left the brigade was deployed: the 122th Illinois, the 89th Indiana, the 58th Illinois, the 21st Missouri, and the 119th Illinois.

13 Ibid., 280, 282, 294.

178th New York was on the right, the 53d Indiana in the right center, the 49th Illinois on the left center, and the 117th Illinois on the left. Lt. John W. Lowell of Battery G, 2d Illinois Light Artillery, had his gunners throw their four pieces into battery in the interval between the 53d Indiana and the 117th Illinois.[14]

Colonel Bouton formed his brigade on the left of Moore's Third Division. The white officers stationed the blacks on a ridge, which sloped to the north, about 1,200 yards south of the field in which the trains were corralled. To protect the army's left flank, Bouton faced his brigade to the south and refused his left regiment—the 68th U.S. Colored Troops. The redlegs of Battery I, 2d U.S. Colored Artillery, unlimbered their four guns on a knoll to the left of the 68th U.S.C.T. The 59th U.S.C.T. was held in reserve; Major Foster formed his people in an open field, with the ground sloping into a thick woods to his front. Bouton covered his battle line with a strong force of skirmishers.[15]

Gilbert's brigade of Moore's Third Division would constitute Smith's ready reserve and guard the trains parked to the south of the Pontotoc road. The brigade commander posted his troops on the left of the train.[16]

One of Grierson's cavalry brigades, Winslow's, was currently engaged in delaying the Rebel build-up west of Harrisburg, while the other, Coon's, was occupying Tupelo and picketing the roads south of Smith's main line of resistance. One cavalry regiment, the 9th Illinois, was not with its brigade. It had been dismounted and posted behind a fence-rail barricade on the left of Bouton's blacks, and

14 Ibid., 280, 295, 296, 299. There was a dense belt of woods about 600 yards in front of the ground defended by the 53d Indiana.

15 Ibid., 302; Cowden, *History of the 59th U.S.C.T.*, 129.

16 *O.R.*, Series I, Vol. 39, pt. 1, 285-286; Scott, *Story of the 32d Iowa*, 291-292. From left to right, Gilbert formed his footsoldiers: the 24th Missouri, and the 27th, 14th and 32d Iowa.

in support of the four guns of Battery I, 2d U.S. Colored Artillery. One battalion of the 9th Illinois was advanced as skirmishers and occupied Thomas's plantation, which was converted into a strongpoint.[17]

The position selected by General A. J. Smith to receive the Confederate attack was well suited for defense. His battleline, forming a right angle several hundred yards north of the Pontotoc road, was on the crest of a low ridge overlooking Harrisburg Branch. From the position held by the 12th Iowa and Murray's brigade, the Federals looked westward toward Pontotoc, the direction from which Generals Lee and Forrest would advance. To the Union front, the terrain sloped gradually down to Harrisburg Branch, beyond which the country was an undulating woodland with scant undergrowth and heavily timbered. From Smith's line, which was slightly over a mile and one-half in length, the distance to the edge of the timber in front varied with the meanders of Harrisburg Branch, which marked the limit of the clearings. Opposite the sector held by Murray's brigade, about 300 yards separated the Union battle line from the timber, but the woods were so open that the Confederates would be visible for the final 500 yards of their approach. Along other sectors of the front, the Rebels, as they advanced to the assault, would be exposed to artillery and small-arms fire for distances varying from one-fourth mile to 1,000 yards.[18]

Generals Lee and Forrest fully appreciated the strength of the Union position and the difficulties that the attacker would face. But they knew that several units of Smith's command had been present at Brice's Crossroads, where they had panicked. If they could penetrate the Union

17 *History of the 9th Illinois Cavalry,* 120; *O.R.,* Series I, Vol. 39, pt. 1, 316, 317.

18 Wyeth, *Life of General N. B. Forrest,* 439; *Atlas to Accompany the Official Records,* Plate LXIII, Fig. 2.

position, there was a good possibility that they could destroy Smith's army. When the two generals discussed the tactical situation about daybreak on July 14, the subject was broached as to whether, under the circumstances, it might not be wiser to postpone the attack until General Smith resumed his march, when they might compel him to accept battle under conditions less disadvantageous to the Confederates. General Lee pointed out to Forrest that it was vital that Smith's column be "dealt with vigorously and at once, so he might" redeploy his forces to reinforce other portions of his department, which were under heavy pressure. According to the latest news from Mobile, Admiral Farragut had increased the strength of his blockading squadron and troops and supplies were being assembled at Pascagoula for an attack on Mobile. General Slocum had advanced out of Vicksburg and was operating against Wirt Adams's outnumbered brigades between the Big Black and Bayou Pierre, and in north Alabama Maj. Gen. Lovell Rousseau was organizing a strong column. Lee admitted that it would be wiser and safer to wait until A. J. Smith was again in motion and then strike, but "it was impossible to say how long the Union commander would remain in his present position," while the threats poised by the other Union columns would not permit delay. Lee was of the opinion that they would have to assail Smith at Harrisburg, or he would be "compelled to withdraw a portion of the troops which were now on the ground and ready for battle . . . to meet the other dangers which were imminent." Forrest, after listening to his superior, agreed, remarking that "all that could be done was to go forward and fight the enemy."[19]

Whether Forrest himself desired to give battle on July 14, 1864, or whether he did so in obedience to the

19 Wyeth, *Life of General N. B. Forrest*, 441-442.

orders of General Lee is open to question. After the battle it was held by Forrest's men that he had merely acquiesced in the fighting of the battle, because Lee had ordered it, and it was generally accepted that Lee had done so because of the pressure upon his department from other Union commands which would require the breakup of the force concentrated to cope with Smith's column.

Forrest never made this excuse in any writing that has been preserved. He noted in his "After Action Report," drafted 17 days after the battle, that "on the morning of the 14th Lt. Gen. Lee ordered the attack to be made, and the troops were disposed for that purpose." As Lee was senior officer, these statements do not necessarily imply any disapproval of the attack on Forrest's part. Many Forrest partisans have maintained that while their champion was no doubt in agreement with the general idea of fighting A. J. Smith, he did object to fighting him at Harrisburg, where the Federals, as Forrest wrote in his "After Action Report," had "overwhelming numbers in an impregnable position."[20]

Maj. Charles W. Anderson, Forrest's assistant adjutant general, recalled that early on the 14th, before the decision to attack was made, Forrest said to Lee:

> The enemy have a strong position--have thrown up defensive works and are vastly our superior in numbers and it will not do for us to attack them under such conditions. One thing sure, the enemy cannot remain long where he is. He must come out, and when he does, all I ask or wish is to be turned loose with my command. I will throw Chalmers' Division on the Ellistown Road, and if Smith undertakes to cross the country to Sherman, turn south to devastate the prairies, or return to Memphis, I will be on all sides of him attacking day and night. He shall not cook a meal

20 Henry, *"First with the Most,"* 316-317.

> or have a night's sleep and I will wear his army to a frazzle before he gets out of the country.[21]

While he did not claim it was a statement voiced by Forrest, Colonel Rucker expressed the opinion that

> had Forrest, and no one else been in command at Harrisburg, he never would have permitted the enemy to get a roasting ear. He would have harassed him so by remaining in his front, flank, and rear, that sooner or later he would have had to make a disastrous retreat. As it was, his retirement was without honor.[22]

General Chalmers on the other hand, in a paper published in the *Southern Historical Society Papers*, two years after Forrest's death, denied that General Stephen D. Lee "made the fight from supposed necessity, and without the concurrance (sic) of General Forrest." Chalmers wrote:

> Lee, Forrest, Buford and I were riding to the front, when the battle was about to begin. Buford said to Lee and Forrest, who had spent the night and morning together in consultation: "Gentlemen, you have not asked my opinion about this fight, but I tell you, we are going to be badly whipped." Forrest replied sharply: "You don't

21 Unpublished Memorandum of 8 pages found in Captain Morton's scrapbooks. This Memorandum was prepared in reply to General Lee's 1902 article in Vol. 6, Publications of the Mississippi Historical Society.

22 Rucker to Morton, Feb. 18, 1902, found in ibid. ||Col. Edmond Winchester Rucker was a native Tennessean, born in 1835. A civil engineer, he had no previous military experience, but he proved to be a highly capable officer. Enlisting in 1861, he eventually raised "Rucker's Legion," an expansion of the 16th Tennessee Cavalry Battalion, in 1863, and served in the Army of Tennessee under Forrest. He was transferred to Mississippi at his own request in early 1864, to follow Forrest, and was assigned a brigade under the Mississippian. One Confederate described Rucker as "formed by nature, except perchance by stature, for a cavalry leader." Bruce S. Allardice, *Confederate Colonels, A Biographical Register* (Columbia, MO: 2008), 329. For Rucker's role at Harrisburg, see Michael P. Rucker, *The Meanest and 'Damnest' Job, The Civil War Experiences and Civilian History of Colonel Edmund Winchester Rucker* (Montgomery, AL: 2019) 168-173.

know what you are talking about; we'll whip 'em in five minutes." Buford replied: "I hope you may be right, but I don't believe it."[23]

Chalmers's statement, however, does not clarify the subject. The decision to attack had been made and Forrest, regardless of what he might have said earlier to Lee, might have been displaying to Buford and the army a show of confidence in its result. The battle having been decided upon, in loyal support of his senior officer, Forrest could hardly have done otherwise.[24]

Writing 37 years after the event, General Lee observed, "Whatever others may say, Gen. Lee and Gen. Forrest were in perfect accord as to delivering battle, and Gen. Forrest personally never shrank from this responsibility before or after the bloody battle."[25]

An air of urgency was added to the situation, Lee recalled, when "two reliable" scouts rode up and reported that the foe was preparing to abandon Tupelo and retreat toward Memphis, via the Ellistown road. Whereupon, Forrest urged an immediate attack, as "his blood was up; the fire of battle was in his eye. He said that if he was in command, he would not hesitate a moment." Whatever the facts as to which of the two generals urged the attack, Lee's recollections as to their leader's military judgment brought forth a storm of protest from Forrest's surviving associates in 1902.[26]

As most of the troops on the field belonged to Forrest's corps and had fought under his leadership at Brice's Crossroads, Lee offered the command to the dynamic Forrest. He declined to assume the responsibility,

23 James R. Chalmers, "Forrest and His Campaigns," *Southern Historical Society Papers*, Vol. 7, 476-477.

24 Henry, *"First With the Most,"* 317.

25 Lee, "Battle of Tupelo," *Publications*, Vol. 6, 45.

26 Ibid., 45; Henry, *"First with the Most,"* 318.

remarking that "Lee was a lieutenant general and therefore his superior, and as such the responsibility was his." Lee replied, "If it is to be a fight, let us fight to the bitter end."[27]

General Lee now gave Forrest his choice as to which wing of the army he would personally direct in the battle. Forrest selected the right, Roddey's division, which was to swing around and envelop Smith's left. Lee would have the Confederate left and center, and assault Mower's division and the right of Moore's. Lee established his command post on the Pontotoc road, near the center of the Confederate line, where he could observe the entire field.[28]

The army reporting to General Lee on the morning of July 14, 1864, numbered about 9,500 effectives, supported by 20 cannon. The composition of this force was: Chalmers's division, McCulloch's and Rucker's brigades, 2,300; Buford's division (Bell's, Crossland's, and Mabry's brigades), 3,200; Roddey's division, Patterson's and Johnson's brigades, 1,500; Beltzhoover's infantry battalion, and the dismounted troopers of Gholson's and Neely's brigades, 2,100; and 360 artillerists. Deducting the horse-holders from the 7,000 cavalry--as they went into the fight dismounted--and including the 2,100 infantry, Lee did not have more than 7,500 effectives available for the fight. The Rebels would be called on to assail the foe in a position of their choosing.[29]

While their skirmishers clashed with Winslow's horsesoldiers west of Harrisburg Branch, the Rebel

27 Lee, "Battle of Tupelo," *Publications*, Vol. 6, 45; Wyeth, *Life of General N. B. Forrest*, 442. | | Parson suggests that Forrest's refusal to take command of the field "must have come as a shock to Lee," since the overwhelming majority of the troops present were in Forrest's own corps. Forrest's sudden refusal is to take command is out of character for the Mississippian, since he usually resented what he viewed as attempts to usurp his authority over his command. Parson, *Work for Giants*, 170.

28 Ibid.

29 Hancock, *Diary*, 421; Wyeth, *Life of General N. B. Forrest*, 442-443.

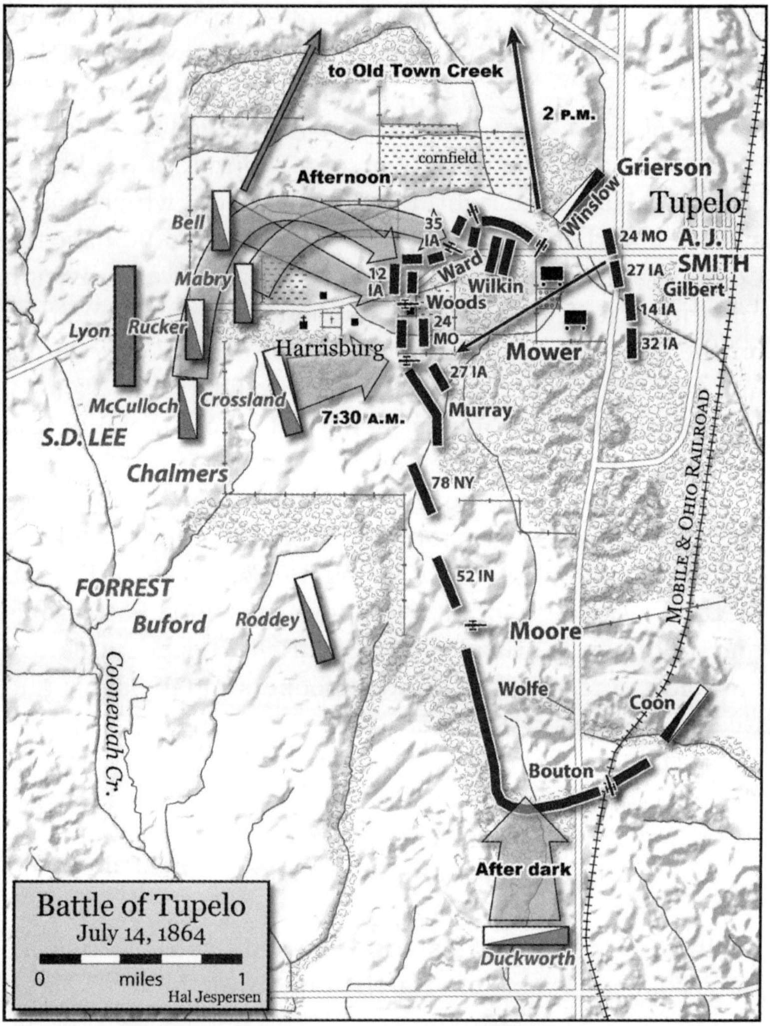

generals deployed their men under the cover of timber. Mabry's brigade was formed on the extreme left, north of the Pontotoc road. Bell's Tennessee Brigade was to the left and rear of Mabry's Mississippians.[30] The Kentucky

30 *O.R.*, Series I, Vol. 39, pt. 1, 347, 349; Hancock, *Diary*, 422. Bell posted the 15th Tennessee on the right of his battle line, the 2d Tennessee on the left, and the 16th Tennessee and Newsom's Regiment in the center.

The heavily outnumbered Confederates attempted to envelop both Federal flanks. Their disjointed and ill-timed attacks, launched one brigade at a time, doomed them to failure.

Brigade, Colonel Crossland commanding, was formed in line of battle on Mabry's right and south of the Pontotoc road.[31] Roddey's two-brigade division was on the right with its right flank refused.[32] The Pettus Flying Artillery was with Roddey's division, while Rice's and Morton's Tennessee batteries were to support Buford's division. Capts. James C. Thrall's Arkansas and Coleman B. Ferrell's Georgia batteries were held in reserve with Chalmers's division. Chalmers massed his people about 400 yards behind Crossland's Kentucky Brigade—Rucker's brigade was to the left and McCulloch's to the right. Farther back near the junction was General Lyon with his 2,100 dismounted cavalry and Beltzhoover's infantry battalion.[33]

By 7 a.m. the Confederates had completed their deployment. Covered by a strong force of skirmishers, their battle lines worked their way through the timber. Having accomplished their mission, Winslow's horsesoldiers pulled back and retired through the picket line held by Crail's battalion. Crail's people delayed the Rebel skirmishers,

31 *O.R.*, Series I, Vol. 39, pt. 1, 336, 338, 340, 341, 342.

32 Hancock, *Diary*, 422, 423. According to James Hancock, one of Roddey's staff officers, the following exchange took place between Generals Lee and Forrest:

General Lee: "Let Roddey's Division form on the left and Buford's on the right."

General Forrest: "No, I want Buford's Division on the left, and Roddey's on the right."

G. L.: "As Roddey is here, who not let him form on the left, and Buford can fall in on the right as he comes up?"

G. F.: "No, I want Buford on the left."

G. L.: "Very well, have your own way then."

33 *O.R.*, Series I, Vol. 39, pt. 1, 322, 326, 334; Wyeth, *Life of General N. B. Forrest*, 443; Hancock, *Diary*, 423.

and only retired when notified by General Smith. As soon as all his men had been recalled, Winslow, in accordance with orders from General Grierson, deployed his brigade, reinforced by the 7th Kansas Cavalry, to guard the army's right and rear.[34] During the afternoon, a battalion of the 7th Kansas under Maj. F. M. Malone rode northward from Tupelo as far as Saltillo, destroying bridges, trestles, and watertanks along the Mobile & Ohio.[35]

General Lee, as he watched the enemy cavalry withdraw through Harrisburg, determined to make a final effort to get the Yankees to abandon the defensive and take the initiative. When Buford's battle line reached the edge of the timber, the troops were halted, while sharpshooters were advanced and the cannoneers of the Pettus Flying Artillery, and Rice's and Morton's batteries unlimbered their guns and opened fire. The Federal redlegs replied. Fully an hour was spent by the Confederates in a futile attempt to draw A. J. Smith from his stronghold, with no benefit other than to focus his attention on the Rebel right. There, about one mile in front of his left wing, he could see Roddey forming his division. Roddey, while Forrest watched, was positioning his people to swing "around on the enemy's left . . . and to advance to the attack." It was at this time that A. J. Smith, concluding that these activities constituted a threat to his left, directed Colonel Moore to call up Wolfe's brigade, while Bouton's blacks and the 9th Illinois Cavalry were thrown into position on Wolfe's left.[36]

By this time it was 8 a.m. There were no clouds in the sky, and the day was already hot. During the past

34 *O.R.* Series I, Vol. 39, pt. 1, 306, 309, 312, 314. The 3d Iowa maintained two picket posts and patrolled the Ellistown road, hourly, to a distance of one and one-fourth miles.

35 Ibid., 319.

36 Ibid., 251; Wyeth, *Life of General N. B. Forrest,* 443-444; Lee, "Battle of Tupelo," *Publications,* Vol. 6, 47-48.

month little rain had fallen in northeast Mississippi and the ground was parched. The blades on the cornstalks were twisted, the leaves were withering, the roads were deep in dust, while many of the smaller streams had ceased to flow. Considerable difficulty was experienced by the company commanders of the two armies in finding sufficient water for their troops to fill canteens.[37]

As the butternuts prepared to advance they faced east, so the morning's sun shone in their eyes, giving many of the Federals the advantage of shooting with their backs to the light. Before passing the order to move out, General Lee had told Forrest to ride to the right, and at the proper moment hurl Roddey's division against Smith's left. Having synchronized their watches, the two generals were in agreement as to the time when the assault was to be made. Forrest, accompanied by his staff, had ridden to join Roddey, who was then nearly a mile to the right. General Lee recalled, "At the expiration of the time agreed upon . . . I ordered the left wing in."[38]

General Buford, whose division constituted the center and left of the Confederate line, received the order to advance and rode with General Lee as far as the edge of "the open space across which in full sweep of the enemy's artillery and small arms his troops must pass before closing in upon them." He now recognized the desperate character of the struggle and the heavy loss of life it would involve. Turning to Lee, he

> modestly expressed the opinion that the attack should not be a direct one, but the majority of the forces should be thrown on the Verona and Tupelo road, and a vigorous assault made on . . . [the foe's] left flank; that a direct charge was what the enemy

37 Wyeth, *Life of General N. B. Forrest*, 444.

38 Ibid.; Lee, "Battle of Tupelo," *Publications*, Vol. 6, 45.

most desired, and for which he was strongly posted both by nature and art.[39]

Buford's advice came too late. The order for the assault had been given, and Forrest had gone off to direct the attack on the right. In Lee's opinion, the battle plan could not be changed.

In moving forward, Crossland obliqued the Kentucky Brigade to the right to regain contact with Roddey, while Mabry's brigade veered to the left. Buford called for Bell to move up into the interval that had opened between Crossland's left and Mabry's right. As chance willed it, the Kentucky Brigade debouched from the timber and entered the cleared fields well in advance of Bell and Mabry. The Kentuckians closed to within 500 yards of the sector of the Union line held by Murray's brigade, before they sighted any bluecoats. Though "ordered to move surely and steadily," Crossland and his regimental commanders found "it was impossible to restrain the ardor" of the men. Believing themselves to be "strongly supported both on the right and left," and raising a shout they charged Murray's line. The Federals held their fire until the onrushing Rebels had closed to within 200 yards, and then they opened "a most terrific fire of artillery and small-arms" on Crossland's people.[40]

39 *O.R.*, Series I, Vol. 39, pt. 1, 330-331.

40 Ibid., 336, 338, 340, 341, 342, 343. The point from which the Kentuckians emerged from the timber was about 800 yards in front of Murray's main line of resistance. Fighting with the Kentucky Brigade this day was a remnant of Brig. Gen. John H. Morgan's command. A month before they had left Cynthiana, Kentucky, after being cut off. Electing Capt. William Campbell to lead them, they started west and south to join Forrest. After bluffing the garrison of Bardstown into surrendering, they pushed on, crossed Green River at Calhoun, forded the Cumberland, and slipped across the Tennessee. Near Corinth, they encountered a detachment of Forrest's scouts. Joining Forrest's corps, Campbell's company was assigned to the

The Fourteenth Wisconsin, of Ward's Brigade, lying prone as they await attack.

William H. Tucker, *The Fourteenth Wisconsin Veteran Volunteer Infantry (General A. J. Smith's Command) in the Expedition and Battle of Tupelo. Indianapolis,* In: F. E. Engle & Son, 1892.

Colonel Murray and his officers kept a tight rein on their men as the Rebels advanced across the fields. Except for the skirmishers and artillerists, the Federals lay on the ground, concealed by the tall corn and bushes. As the Kentuckians began to close in, Murray saw that their line of battle extended "nearly to the extreme left of my position, in our front being an extensive and open, cleared field, giving us a view of the approaching line."

The cannoneers of the 3d Indiana Battery, manning the three guns in the interval between the 122d Illinois and 89th Indiana, had been, since 7 o'clock, employing their James rifle to duel with the artillery to their front. Lieutenant Burns now shouted for his gunners to switch from shell to canister and turn their pieces on the Confederates sweeping toward them. Lieutenant McPherson's crew, serving the 6-pounder James Rifle on

Kentucky Brigade. Memoirs of John N. Johnson of Dublin, Virginia, found in the Tennessee State Library.

the right of the 122d Illinois, likewise changed targets. Worse, if possible, for the Confederates, Lt. John W. Lowell of Battery G, 2d Illinois Light Artillery, saw that there was no threat to the front held by Wolfe's brigade, and he had his redlegs change front to the right to command the fields in front of Murray's brigade. As Crossland swept closer, Lowell's cannoneers "opened a destructive cross-fire upon his lines," first with shell, and then as the range shortened, with canister.[41]

The enfilading fire of Lowell's and McPherson's five guns was "most destructive" to Crossland's line. Roddey's division had failed to advance, and this failure had drawn on the right flank of the Kentucky Brigade a storm of canister that, in Crossland's words, "was fatal to my men." Realizing that to retreat would be more dangerous than to go on, Crossland rode out in front and shouted, "Forward men; forward!" The line wavered for a moment, but the men, after a momentary pause, rushed on, "intent upon carrying the enemy's works and driving him before them."

When the Kentuckians charged to within 50 to 100 yards, the Union regimental commanders, in compliance with Murray's orders, called for their men "to rise up and advance." Murray's people sprang to their feet, "and with a yell like that of demons," let go a crashing volley right into the Kentuckians' faces. Crossland's ranks were decimated; his men mowed down. Many of the best officers were killed or wounded. Col. W. W. Faulkner of the 12th Kentucky Cavalry had his horse killed by a shell from Battery G, which also seriously wounded him. Faulkner, however, refused to turn back, and advanced until struck a second time. Maj. Thomas S. Tate pushed forward the regiment's left battalion until some of the men were within 30 yards of the Federal line. Pvt. A. P. Hill of

41 *O.R.*, Series I, Vol. 39, pt. 1, 280, 282, 294, 299.

Company E was killed within 20 steps of Murray's main line of resistance. Ensign G. W. Dunn was cut down as he carried the colors of the 12th forward. Capt. J. F. Melton snatched them from under his body and bore them the remainder of the fight. After the battle, it was found that the flag had been shredded by 18 bullets or jagged iron fragments from bursting shells. Tate now heard the men crying that the regiment on the right was retreating, and on glancing in that direction he saw a unit falling back in wild disorder. He bellowed for the left battalion of the 12th Kentucky to fall back, as he dashed to the right to rally the men in that sector. One regiment, the 8th Kentucky Mounted Infantry, took even worse punishment, losing one-half its men killed or wounded within a few minutes.[42]

As if the frontal fire of Murray's brigade and the four guns of the 3d Indiana Battery were not bad enough, Crossland's right and center were ripped by crashing volleys from Colonel Wolfe's right flank regiments—the 52d Indiana and 178th New York. These units were positioned to punish the Rebels from the right oblique.[43]

The charge of Murray's bluecoats, supported on the left by the 52d Indiana, was too much for any force that had been punished so severely to withstand. Many of the Kentuckians were heard to cry in despair, as they fled, "My God! My God!" Murray's grim footsoldiers hounded the Rebels as they retreated, "pouring deadly volleys into their rapidly thinning ranks." After pursuing the Kentuckians about 350 yards to the foot of the ridge in front of where they had met the attack, Murray and his regimental

42 Ibid., 336, 338, 340, 343. Lt. Lowell of Battery G claimed for his unit the credit of doing "the enemy more damage than all the other five [batteries] combined." He was watching when one of his projectiles struck Colonel Faulkner's "splendid charger," wounding the colonel and killing the horse. Ibid., 298-299.

43 Ibid., 295, 297, 298, 299.

commanders halted and re-formed their units. While doing so, they continued to fire at will on "the scattered fugitives." The last of the butternuts had disappeared into the timber to their front, when the Federals, in obedience to orders from Colonel Moore, retired in good order to their original positions on the ridge east of Harrisburg. Murray's right flank regiment, the 122d Illinois, which had advanced across a cornfield to a fence fronting the church and other buildings in the deserted village, was not recalled. Taking cover behind the fence, the regiment prepared to support the troops of Mower's division posted north of the Pontotoc road.[44]

General Forrest at the time of Crossland's advance was with General Roddey. After giving Roddey his orders to swing his troops around the enemy's left, Forrest rode forward to select "a position in which to place his troops." But on reaching the front, he looked to the left and was shocked to see the Kentucky Brigade fleeing. Putting the spurs to his horse, he rode to the left, rushed in among the retreating troops, seized a stand of colors, and rallied them at the edge of the timber.

Roddey's division having failed to close with the foe in time to support Crossland's assault, Forrest turned it back when it came up, because "the terrific fire poured upon the gallant Kentucky brigade showed that the enemy were supported by overwhelming numbers in an impregnable position."[45] As soon as Crossland's men had

44 Ibid., 280, 282-283, 284, 285, 295, 297. After retiring to the ridge, at least one of Murray's regimental commanders, Col. Thomas J. Kinney of the 119th Illinois, shielded his front with skirmishers, and went out with the hospital corps to look after the wounded. "While engaged in this humane act of administering to the wounded rebels on the field, . . . [they] were fired upon by the enemy from the woods, some 300 yards distant. This caused . . . [them] to cease . . . [their] kindness for a time." Ibid., 284.

45 Ibid., 322, 336; Wyeth, *Life of General N. B. Forrest,* 449-450; Lee, "Battle of Tupelo," *Publications,* Vol. 6, 47-48.

been re-formed and rested, they were ordered by General Lee to retire and help cover the Tupelo-Verona road.

Colonel Wolfe and the cannoneers of Battery G, 2d Illinois Light Artillery, had watched as Roddey's battle line came into view on the opposite ridge. The rout of Crossland's brigade had deprived the redlegs of targets, so Lieutenant Lowell was delighted when General Smith sent word for him to shift one of his sections farther to the left. After the gunners had got off a few rounds, Roddey, in accordance with orders from Forrest, moved back and formed line of battle covering the Tupelo-Verona road, while the cannoneers of Ferrell's Battery and the Pettus Flying Artillery unlimbered their guns. Lieutenant Lowell now advanced his second section and dueled with the two Rebel batteries. The Confederate smoothbores soon ceased fire, but their rifled guns continued to boom.[46]

In response to orders from Colonel Moore, two regiments, the 24th Missouri and 27th Iowa, were called up from the reserve to support Murray's brigade. Arriving at the front, these regiments took position about 60 yards in rear of the 3d Indiana Battery.[47]

Meanwhile, General Buford, seeing that the Kentucky Brigade by its rash advance was faced with disaster, hastened forward Mabry and Bell to strike the right of Smith's line and create a diversion. Mabry's advance was on the oblique to the left, and in passing through the woods, his Mississippians gained the cleared fields well in advance of Bell's Tennesseans, who had not yet left the timber. Mabry and his men saw that the Federals to their front were posted on either side of the Pontotoc road, with their right refused. Some of the Union regiments, it was seen, had strengthened their position on the crest

46 *O.R.*, Series I, Vol. 39, pt. 1, 299, 322.

47 *O.R.*, Series I, Vol. 39, pt. 1, 286, 292; Scott, *Story of the 32d Iowa*, 292.

by throwing down rail fences. The ground across which they would have to advance to come to grips with soldiers of Woods's and Ward's brigades was open and "gently undulating, affording no protection" to the attacker. Mabry, in view of the disaster that had overtaken Crossland, did not wait for Bell's people to come up on his right, but called for an advance.

The Mississippians stormed forward, driving in Mower's skirmishers. As soon as they debouched from the woods, the butternuts drew the fire of the guns manned by the cannoneers of the 2d Iowa and 6th Indiana Batteries. Mabry's dismounted horsesoldiers closed to within 300 yards of Mower's main line of resistance, and "received a most terrific fire of small-arms." Mabry bellowed, "Charge!" An advance across open fields, swept by exploding shells, canister, and minie balls, on a hot sultry morning had taken a heavy toll. The fainthearted had skulked, reducing the brigade to little more than a skirmish line. Even so, Mabry and his Mississippians drove to within about 60 yards of the bluecoated infantry. Seeing that his line was too much weakened to drive the foe, Mabry halted and had his men take cover in a hollow and behind a low fence. Here they hugged the ground and banged away.[48]

The historian of the 12th Iowa recalled that he and his comrades, as they crouched behind their fence-rail barricade, could see the Rebel battle line sweeping toward them. Despite the knowledge that they would be called on to bear the brunt of the assault, they held their fire until the butternuts had advanced to within easy range, when "they opened fire with a coolness and accuracy which was only excelled by the rapidity with which they discharged and reloaded their muskets." Not a man wavered or fell back; those killed or severely wounded lay where they fell,

48 *O.R.*, Series I, Vol. 39, pt. 1, 331, 349.

unheeded by their comrades. Those less seriously injured, who were able to get to the rear unaided, left weapons and cartridges with their buddies, and made their way to the field hospital.[49]

Woods's and Ward's infantry had punished the Mississippians unmercifully, before Bell's Tennesseans came up on the double and took position to their right and rear. A soldier in the 2d Tennessee reported, "Never had such an appalling fire of musketry and artillery blazed and gushed in the face" of our regiment. Not a man, however, hesitated. Colonel Barteau was wounded when within 20 yards of the Federals' works. Many of Mabry's men took advantage of Bell's advance to slip to the rear. Bell's brigade secured ground within 75 yards of the position defended by the 12th Iowa and 33d Missouri and took cover. A deadly fire-fight ensued.[50]

General A. J. Smith wrote that when they left the cover of the timber, the Confederate lines "could be distinguished separately, but as they advanced they lost all semblance of lines and the attack resembled a mob of huge magnitude." There was "no skirmish line or main line or reserve, but seemed to be a foot race to see who should reach us first. They were allowed to approach, yelling and howling like Comanches, to within canister range, when the batteries" opened upon them.[51] Next came a crashing volley. The Confederates were pinned down. In the fight which ensued great quantities of ammunition were expended. After a while soldiers of the 12th Iowa raised the cry that they were running short of cartridges and their rifle-muskets were becoming foul. Colonel Woods called up the 7th Minnesota. The Iowans, with the exception of Companies

49 Reed, *The 12th Iowa*, 155-156.

50 *O.R.*, Series I, Vol. 39, pt. 1, 347; Hancock, *Diary*, 423-425.

51 *O.R.*, Series I, Vol. 39, pt. 1, 252.

COL. ALEXANDER WILKIN

Wilkin, of the 9th Minnesota Infantry, was the highest ranking Federal killed at Tupelo.

Minnesota Historical Society

E and H, changed places with the Minnesotans.[52]

From their position behind the fences east of Harrisburg, the 122d Illinois was able to catch Bell's Tennesseans, as they charged Woods's brigade, in a murderous crossfire. The cannoneers of the 3d Indiana Battery, the foe to their front having disappeared, hammered away at the Confederates north of the Pontotoc road. In a futile effort to nullify this fire, sharpshooters infiltrated the village and occupied positions in and about the church.[53]

General Mower, at the beginning of the attack, told Colonel Wilkin to have two regiments, the 47th Illinois and the 11th Missouri, form on the right of the train to shield it from an attack from the northeast. After Wilkin had positioned these regiments, he rejoined his brigade. Just as he reached his right flank, he was struck by a minie ball and killed. Thus died the highest ranking Union officer to meet death on the field. The next senior officer in the unit, Col. John O. McClure of the 47th Illinois, assumed

52 Ibid., 270, 272; Reed, *The 12th Iowa*, 156. Companies E and H, having been supplied with cartridges, were allowed to remain at the front with the Minnesotans. Banks's and Hoag's companies of the 7th Minnesota, which had been at the front with the 12th Iowa, likewise were retired to draw ammunition.

53 *O.R.*, Series I, Vol. 39, pt. 1, 283.

command of the Eagle Brigade.[54] Colonel Gilbert, acting upon instructions from General Smith, now crossed the Pontotoc road with the 14th and 32d Iowa and posted them on the right of the 11th Missouri. By this move, Smith had committed the last of his ready reserve.[55]

Covered by Bell's brigade, Mabry withdrew his shattered command. His losses in the hollow had been devastating. His horse had been killed near the foe, so Mabry had to delegate to two of his staff—Capt. J. R. Chambers and Lt. W. H. Gee.[56] As the Mississippians were retiring, they encountered an advancing battle line—Rucker's.

General Chalmers, after the battle had been joined, was confused to receive three different orders. From General Forrest came word to move to the right and support Roddey; from General Lee to move to the left to reinforce Mabry; and from Buford "an order stating that I should move, by direction of General Lee, to relieve him on the center." Forrest being his immediate superior, Chalmers obeyed his instructions and led his division toward the right. But before he reached Roddey's command post, General Lee overtook him and told Chalmers to divide his

54 Ibid., 265-266; Bryner, *Bugle Echoes*, 132. To cover the corral a line of skirmishers was thrown out to its front, while the regiments were formed into line on its right.

55 *O.R.*, Series I, Vol. 39, pt. 1, 286, 289, 291; Scott, *Story of the 32d Iowa*, 292. One of the soldiers in the 32d Iowa recalled that soon after receipt of Smith's orders to move to the right, an orderly rode up with instructions for Gilbert to advance to "the support of the center, or it must be broken." Gilbert replied, "I have an order from General Smith to hold this point at all hazards, and leave it for no man's order, save his own, and hold it I will." After crossing the Pontotoc road, Gilbert posted the 32d Iowa on the right and the 14th Iowa on the left.

56 *O.R.*, Series I, Vol. 39, pt. 1, 349-350. Col. Isham Harrison and Lt. Col. Thomas M. Nelson of the 6th Mississippi Cavalry, and Maj. Robert C. McCay of the 38th Mississippi Mounted Infantry had been slain; Lt. Col. John Cage of the 14th Confederate Cavalry mortally wounded; and Lt. Col. Thomas R. Stockdale of the 4th Mississippi Cavalry injured.

unit. McCulloch's brigade would be held in reserve, while Rucker's marched to the left with the orders "to charge at a double-quick and with a shout."[57]

Chalmers accompanied Rucker. Crossing the Pontotoc road, Rucker formed his brigade into line of battle. The marching and counter-marching in the heat, while the generals made up their minds, had taken a toll. Rucker's brigade was jaded by the time it crossed to the north of the Pontotoc road; a number of men had straggled. When the brigade moved forward, Rucker rode on the left and Chalmers on the right. They "passed over plowed ground and through a corn-field, in full view of the enemy, strongly posted on an elevated and wooded ridge." Before they "reached the position to charge many of the men fainted from exhaustion." Up the grade the brigade charged by the right flank, "the men falling everywhere from the murderous fire of the enemy's infantry." Passing through the remnants of Mabry's brigade which were being withdrawn, Rucker's grim fighters continued their surge. Rucker was hit twice and carried from the field badly wounded. As soon as Rucker's people came up on their left, Bell's Tennesseans pulled back from the ground they had gained within 75 yards of the right angle in Woods's line, "leaving a good many of our dead and wounded on the field." In the words of Colonel Bell, "the place was truly a hot one, and the enemy's position strong and commanding, well selected, and well fortified. The loss of the brigade in killed and wounded . . . was immense."

57 || Forrest erred badly here. Forrest had voluntarily relinquished command over Chalmers that morning; leaving Lee in direct command. Now Forrest meddled in that chain of command, distracting and disrupting the Confederate attack at a crucial moment, and ultimately, leading to the fracturing of Chalmers's division into a series of piecemeal movements. Parson, *Work for Giants*, 203.

Col. William L. Duckworth of the 7th Tennessee Cavalry, who succeeded Rucker, sought to rally the brigade and continue the fight. He saw Color Sgt. Egbert Shepherd of his regiment shot down. "Save the flag!" cried one of the desperately wounded, and a dozen men rushed forward to grasp and uphold the treasured symbol. A member of Company E reached it first. After an "ineffectual effort" to carry the sector of the Union line held by Ward's brigade, supported on the left by the 35th Iowa and 33d Missouri, Rucker's people retreated into a hollow which afforded some protection and re-formed.[58]

When Rucker's brigade stormed forward, Colonel McMillen had called for his left flank regiment, the 10th Minnesota, to wheel to the left and to extend Ward's line. The position occupied by the regiment was screened from Chalmers's view by the crest of the ridge on which were emplaced the Rodman rifles manned by the 6th Indiana Battery. Lt. Col. S. P. Jennison held his men there until he was satisfied that Rucker's people were within range. At a word from their colonel, the Minnesotans "rose as one man . . . and gave them a volley, which was the last they waited to receive that day."[59]

The Confederate artillerists, though outgunned by the Federal redlegs, did their best to support the futile assaults of the dismounted horsesoldiers. As the brigades were forming in the woods, two of the batteries, the Pettus Flying Artillery on the extreme right with its section of 10-pounder Parrotts and Thrall's on the Pontotoc road with its four 6-pounder guns, had dueled with the 3d Indiana and Battery G. When the Rebel battle lines swept forward, these daring cannoneers advanced their eight

58 Ibid., 326, 247; Lee "Battle of Tupelo," *Publications*, Vol. 46; Young, *7th Tennessee Cavalry*, 97-99.

59 *O.R.*, Series I, Vol. 39, pt. 1, 264. The line of the 10th Minnesota overlapped Rucker's to a considerable distance.

guns. Rice's Battery moved in support of Crossland's Kentuckians and unlimbered its four 6-pounders north of the road. On the left, Morton's Battery commanded by Lt. T. Sanders Sale took position with its four 3-inch rifles in rear of Mabry's and Bell's brigades. Sale, advancing boldly, threw his pieces into battery within 400 yards of Mower's battle line. Here his gunners fought the redlegs of the 2d Iowa and 6th Indiana Batteries. Five out of the seven men and six of the eight horses assigned to one of Sale's rifles were disabled, and the gun captain, Sergeant Brown, three times wounded. He refused to abandon the piece, and remained with it until it was manhandled from the field by Captain Titus's company of sharpshooters. Another gun was brought off by Sgt. C. T. Brady, after a wheel had been shattered.

After covering the retreat of the dismounted cavalry, the Rebel artillery limbered to the rear to save their guns. In the artillery duels, only one Union battery, the 3d Indiana, received much punishment as they commanded the field.[60]

General Mower, seeing that Rucker's brigade was starting to give ground, ordered his brigade commanders to advance and mop-up the Confederates to their front. The fight had lasted about 150 minutes, when Colonel Woods on the right waved his men forward.[61] On the left, next to the Pontotoc road, the 12th Iowa moved out, supported by the 7th Minnesota. The Iowans obliqued to the left and the Minnesotans to the right. The 33d Missouri and the 35th Iowa advanced on the right of the Minnesota regiment. Ward's brigade swept into position on Woods's right, while

60 Wyeth, *Life of General N. B. Forrest*, 448; Hancock, *Diary*, 426-427; *O.R.*, Series I, Vol. 39, pt. 1, 294, 334.

61 By this time, the soldiers of the eight companies of the 7th Minnesota on the firing line had exhausted their ammunition, and they, in turn, had been relieved by the 12th Iowa and Banks's and Hoag's companies of the 7th Minnesota. *O.R.*, Series I, Vol. 39, pt. 1, 272; Reed, *The 12th Iowa*, 156.

Colonel McClure with the 9th Minnesota and detachments of the 5th Minnesota and 8th Wisconsin moved up from the reserve and fell in on Ward's right.

Woods's and Ward's bluecoats, as they advanced, captured a number of prisoners and smashed at least one pocket of resistance. Company D, 33d Missouri, came upon a party of Rebel sharpshooters and overwhelmed them, capturing the colors of the 6th Mississippi Cavalry. On the left, the Yankees followed the retreating Confederates about 500 yards; McClure's men on the right advanced about two-thirds of a mile before they came up on line with Woods's and Ward's people.

Mower, seeing that the foe had fallen back on their horseholders, called a halt, as two of his field officers and several of his men had been sunstruck. Like the Americans in Vietnam, A. J. Smith called for a body count. His subordinates reported that there were 270 Rebel dead on the field in front of Mower's position. The Confederate wounded were gathered up and taken to the field hospital the Federals had established to care for their injured. Lacking transportation to remove the small-arms abandoned by the enemy, Smith had his men collect them and smash the stocks of the rifle-muskets against trees. After his people had policed the field and rounded-up Confederate prisoners, Mower, satisfied that Generals Lee and Forrest were unlikely to resume the offensive, had his brigades return to the positions occupied prior to the charge.[62]

McCulloch's brigade, at the time of Rucker's assault, had moved forward and relieved the terribly mauled Kentucky Brigade. General Lee now saw that the Union left was not engaged, and suspecting that something had gone wrong with the Confederate battle plan, he rode

62 *O.R.*, Series I, Vol. 39, pt. 1, 252, 257-258, 266, 267, 270, 271, 272-273, 274-275, 277; Reed, *The 12th Iowa*, 156-157; Bryner, *Bugle Echoes*, 132.

MAJ. GEN. STEPHEN D. LEE

Lee commanded the Rebel forces at Tupelo.

Library of Congress

to the right. He soon encountered General Forrest and inquired, "Why did you not carry out the plan of attack?"

Forrest answered, because "Buford's right [the Kentucky Brigade] had been rashly thrown forward and repulsed," and "in the exercise of my discretion I did not move Roddey forward, but I have moved him to the left, and formed a new line."

"In doing as you did," Lee snapped, "you failed to carry out the plan of battle agreed on." As it was now too late to turn the tide of battle, Lee explained, he had ordered McCulloch to hold his ground and cover the withdrawal of the four battered brigades—Crossland's, Mabry's, Bell's, and Rucker's.[63]

The Confederate leaders were delighted when the Federals failed to exploit the disaster. About 1 p.m. General Lee directed Forrest to recall his corps and take position at Mrs. Sample's. There Forrest redeployed Chalmers's and Buford's divisions, reinforced by Lyon's infantry division, into line of battle fronting several large cleared fields. Although the position selected was a formidable one, Forrest had his people strengthen it further by throwing up temporary breastworks of rails, logs, and cotton bales. With their artillery unlimbered and trained to command the approaches to Mrs. Sample's, the Confederate leaders "anxiously awaited" the Yankees.

Crossland's brigade was detached and reinforced Roddey's division and Ferrell's Battery on the Tupelo-Verona road. This was done to prevent the foe from advancing on Okolona and stealing a march toward Columbus and the Black Prairie Region. In compliance with instructions from General Roddey, Crossland's Kentuckians established a roadblock, one and a half miles north of Verona.[64]

A. J. Smith was a capable but overly cautious officer. After checking with his principal subordinates and learning that their men had been exhausted by the hard-marches and heat, and that rations were running

63 Lee, "Battle of Tupelo," *Publications*, Vol. 6, 46-47.

64 *O.R.*, Series I, Vol. 39, pt. 1, 322-323, 326-327, 331, 336, 339, 343; Hancock, *Diary*, 428. Bell's brigade early in the afternoon was permitted to retire to Calhoun's Crossroads to draw forage and rations from the corps' trains.

short, he determined not to exploit the morning's success. Orders were issued for the troops to hold their ground and strengthen their positions in case the foe renewed the attack.[65]

The only action that occurred along the front defended by the bluecoated infantry during the afternoon was on the extreme left. Bouton's brigade on that flank found itself harassed by Roddey's sharpshooters ensconced in the woods to its front. To cope with this threat, Bouton twice took forward a section of Battery I, 2d U.S. Colored Artillery, and shelled the foe from the timber. Troopers of the 9th Illinois Cavalry, covering the ground to Bouton's left, were engaged in continuous skirmishing with combat patrols pushed forward by Roddey. About 5:30 Bouton reported that the Confederates were in force on the Verona road, and to cope with this threat A. J. Smith ordered Gilbert's brigade to that sector. Gilbert marched his troops cross-country and formed them on the left of Bouton's brigade, where they took position "behind the crest of a high hill, which commanded the whole field." Skirmishers were advanced and occupied the next ridge.[66]

No attack developing, Smith recalled Bouton's and Gilbert's brigades. The brigade commanders, after detailing a strong force of skirmishers to hold the ground, assembled and marched their troops back to their camps, one-half mile to the rear. The messes were turned to preparing the evening's rations. The 9th Illinois Cavalry,

65 *O.R.*, Series I, Vol. 39, pt. 1, 252.

66 Ibid., 286, 290, 291, 292, 317; Cowden, *History of the 59th U.S.C.T.*, 129. At 10:30 the 24th Missouri of Gilbert's brigade had been redeployed from its position in support of the 3d Indiana Battery and placed between Murray's and Wolfe's brigades, where it remained until 5:30 p.m. when it rejoined its parent unit.

except one battalion assigned to patrol in front of the infantry, rejoined Coon's brigade.[67]

Earlier in the day, there had been some activity south and east of Tupelo which caused General Grierson a few anxious moments, before he learned of their limited scope. Shortly after daybreak, Captain Tyler's combat patrol (which had spent the night at Verona) had advanced up the Tupelo road. Tyler was supported by Moreland's Alabama Cavalry Regiment of Roddey's division. Two and one-half miles south of Tupelo, Union pickets were encountered. Quickly dismounting, the Rebels advanced on the double and drove the foe back one-half mile to Thomas's plantation, where his support was posted, a battalion of the 9th Illinois. Alerted by the retreat of their comrades, the Yanks took cover in the buildings and behind fences. Tyler posted his men behind the crest of a hill within 300 yards of the buildings. A severe fire-fight ensued. Maj. J. N. George of Moreland's Regiment refused to come to the Kentuckians support, and Tyler deemed it imprudent, because of the smallness of his command, to charge.

Receiving a message from General Lee to watch the foe's movements, Tyler recalled his men and returned to Verona. He then crossed Oldtown Creek, and occupied the levee east of Tupelo. His men, taking advantage of the Federals' preoccupation with Lee and Forrest, occupied all the bridges, except the one across the slough. Grierson, over-estimating the strength of Tyler's patrol, had the slough bridge burned, and deployed a strong force along its bank to prevent a dash into Tupelo by the Rebels.[68]

During the afternoon General Smith sought Grierson's help in ascertaining the foe's whereabouts. Grierson ordered out two battalions of cavalry, one each from the

67 *O.R.*, Series I, Vol. 39, pt. 1, 286, 293, 302, 317.

68 Ibid., 345.

3d and 4th Iowa, under Maj. George Duffield. Duffield's column rode out the Pontotoc road, and, after a two mile advance, the bluecoats reined up their horses upon sighting Forrest's fortified position at Mrs. Sample's. While the Federals were deploying into line, they came under fire from one of the Rebel batteries, and an exploding shell wounded four troopers of the 3d Iowa. Duffield, having satisfied himself that the foe was present in force, returned to report what he had seen to General Smith. Before reaching Harrisburg, Duffield detached three companies of the 3d Iowa (D, L, and M) with orders to picket the Pontotoc road and sound the alarm should the foe attempt a night attack.[69]

Lee and Forrest became impatient as the hours passed, and the Federals made no move to press their advantage. The Confederates' ire was aroused when the enemy at dark commenced burning Harrisburg. Chalmers now moved forward with McCulloch's brigade, some skirmishers of the 1st Mississippi Infantry, and one gun. He was to make a forced reconnaissance of the Union position flanking the Pontotoc road. Forrest at the same time rode out with Rucker's brigade (now led by Colonel Duckworth) to feel A. J. Smith's left.[70]

Chalmers's column found Woods's and Murray's brigades strongly posted on the ridge east of Harrisburg.

69 Ibid., 306, 309-310; Scott, *Story of a Cavalry Regiment*, 288.

70 *O.R.*, Series I, Vol. 39, pt. 1, 323, 327; Hancock, *Diary*, 428; Lee, "Battle of Tupelo," *Publications*, Vol. 6, 48; Young, *7th Tennessee Cavalry*, 99. Harrisburg was already a dying town, doomed by the railroad, as the business houses had been moved to Tupelo in 1860. The first settlement had been made in 1847 by G. C. Thomason, who opened a store on land purchased from Judge W. R. Harris, a wealthy planter. By 1853 Harrisburg boasted three stores, a Methodist church, a Masonic Lodge, a blacksmith shop, and a school. A post office was established in 1851 with John Long as postmaster. Before the opening of the railroad to Tupelo in 1860, Harrisburg had a population of nearly 100. Franklin L. Riley, "Extinct Towns and Villages of Mississippi," *Publications*, Vol. 5, 351-352.

The cannoneers threw their gun into battery, while the soldiers of the 1st Mississippi clashed with Union pickets. Taking advantage of the glow from the fires engulfing Harrisburg, the artillerists hurled a number of shells into the Union lines.

Meanwhile, Forrest was leading Rucker's brigade on a march to the southeast. The Confederates gained the Union left. Here Duckworth, under Forrest's watchful eye, dismounted and deployed his brigade across the Tupelo-Verona road. At a word from Forrest, the brigade attacked and rolled back the picket line manned by Bouton's and Gilbert's brigades. At the first outcry, Bouton and Gilbert had the "long roll" beaten and their brigades turned out on the double. Wolfe's brigade, which had remained on the line, was waiting for the Confederates. The 117th Illinois, Wolfe's left flank regiment, sent volley after volley crashing into the darkness. Bouton's blacks came up on the double with fixed bayonet, while Gilbert deployed his men on the run. Forrest recalled that the fire which these three brigades opened on us was "one of the heaviest . . . I have heard during the war. There was unceasing roar of small-arms, and his whole line was lighted up by a continuous stream of fire." As the Federals were on a ridge and the Rebels in the hollows, they made an error characteristic of night actions by shooting too high, and none of the men with Forrest were killed.[71]

Having stirred up the Yankees and made certain there would be little sleep in their camps, Forrest recalled Rucker's brigade and Chalmers. On returning to Mrs. Sample's, Forrest ordered Buford to turn out his division and ride to the right and reinforce Roddey's troops holding

71 *O.R.*, Series I, Vol. 39, pt. 1, 281, 286, 295, 302, 323, 327; Hancock, *Diary*, 426-429; Young, *7th Tennessee Cavalry*, 99; Cowden, *History of the 59th U.S.C.T.*, 129-130. The Confederates drove back Bouton's and Gilbert's picket lines about 1,300 yards.

the Tupelo-Verona road. Bell's brigade accordingly marched from Palmetto Church to Dr. Calhoun's, where it arrived shortly after daybreak. Mabry's brigade remained where it was, and a regiment, the 14th Confederate, was detached and advanced to harass the bluecoats in front of the fire-blackened ruins marking the site of Harrisburg.[72]

The Federal infantry, following Forrest's night attack, was not allowed to return to its camps, and the army rested on its arms. Around the camp fires the talk was whether the next day, July 15, would bring another battle or find them in pursuit of the defeated Rebels.[73]

In the fight on July 14 there were seven mounted Confederate brigades on the field, and of these three were not closely engaged. Deducting horse-holders, the four brigades which assailed Smith's infantry in succession were able to field about 3,800 effectives, counting the supporting artillery. Their reported losses were 1,249 killed or wounded, with another 49 missing, or slightly over 34 percent. Few, if any, mounted commands suffered as frightful casualties during the war. Buford's division lost 22 officers killed and 104 wounded; 131 enlisted men killed, 694 wounded, and 49 missing, for a total of 1,000 in the Tupelo Campaign. Most of these casualties were suffered on July 14. In seven of Buford's regiments, every field officer was a casualty. One command, the 2d Tennessee, came out of the fight led by Lt. George Seay. The four brigades had gone into action piecemeal and had been slaughtered. Never again would these four units be capable of mounting an effective assault on a Union position—their combat effectiveness had been destroyed.[74]

72 *O.R.*, Series I, Vol. 39, pt. 1, 323, 331, 237, 350.

73 Ibid., 286, 295-296, 302,303; Scott, *Story of a Cavalry Regiment*, 288-289.

74 Hancock, *Diary*, 434-435.

CAPT. JOHN W. MORTON

Morton wanted to mass his guns for a bombardment along the Pontotoc Road before the dismounted cavalry charged.

Tennessee State Library and Archives

General Forrest, when he filed his "After Action Report" on August 1, made no apologies or explanation, beyond the statement that while he was positioning Roddey's division on the right, Crossland's Kentucky Brigade was "rashly precipitated forward." In Jordan and Pryor's account, which Forrest saw and approved, it was said:

> General Lee's orders really were that his centre should stand still, while the right (Roddey) should have time to swing around into a position as near to the enemy as that held by Buford, but from a misunderstanding, the Kentucky brigade prematurely began the attack.[75]

Stephen D. Lee, because of his departure to command a corps in the Army of Tennessee, made no "After Action Report." Thirty-seven years later, after a distinguished career as an educator and leader of the United Confederate Veterans, he charged that General Forrest changed the battle plan by not ordering Roddey forward "at the signal agreed on."

General Lee, he wrote, using the third person:

75 Jordan & Pryor, *Forrest and His Campaigns*, 508.

> moved to the right, to see what was the cause. He soon met Gen. Forrest, and said to him: "Why did you not carry out the plan of attack?" Forrest replied: "Buford's right had been rashly thrown forward and repulsed. In the exercise of my discretion I did not move Roddey forward, but I have moved him to the left, and formed a new line." Gen. Lee said: "In doing as you did, you failed to carry out the plan of battle agreed on."[76]

Forrest's surviving associates took exception to Lee's statement. Interpreting his statements as an attack on their hero, they pointed out that no provision had been made for the discharge of a cannon to signal when the attack was to commence. Lee's tactics were likewise assailed. Captain Morton, Forrest's chief of artillery, claimed that before the battle, he had urged Lee to permit him to mass his 20 guns on either side of the Pontotoc road and hammer the Federal positions to the immediate front. Such a bombardment, he reasoned, would soften up this sector of the line and make it vulnerable to attack. Lee vetoed his suggestion, and the five Confederate batteries were scattered.[77]

While the grizzled veterans battled away with pen and ink, it should be observed that friendship between Forrest and Lee remained unbroken until Forrest's death, for as Lee wrote of the mismanagement of the Confederate officers on the field of Harrisburg, "I am sure he [Forrest] did the best as he saw it. I am sure I did my best as I saw it."[78]

76 Lee, "Battle of Tupelo," *Publications*, Vol. 6, 45-47.

77 Morton, *Artillery of Nathan Bedford Forrest*, 207-208.

78 Henry, *"First With the Most,"* 324.

5

A. J. Smith Retires and the Fight at Oldtown Creek

ON THE morning of July 15, 1864, General A. J. Smith received disturbing information from his chief of commissary. He was told that most of the hardtack had spoiled, and the army had on hand but one day's ration. The chief of ordnance had more bad news—after issuing all the reserve artillery ammunition there were only about 100 rounds per gun. After evaluating the reports regarding the foe, in view of this intelligence, Smith determined that rather than attempt to force the Rebels into another engagement, he would return to Memphis. Orders were given for the infantry to hold its ground, while the wounded Confederates, along with 40 of the most seriously injured Federals, were transferred into Tupelo for hospitalization. Two surgeons, with medical supplies to last for ten days, were detailed to remain with the wounded, along with a number of enlisted men as male nurses.[1]

Orders in the meantime were given for General Grierson to put his cavalry in motion. Winslow's brigade was to execute a forced reconnaissance out the Pontotoc road to see if the foe was still in position at Mrs. Sample's, and to bring off a cannon which had been disabled and abandoned

1 *O.R.*, Series I, Vol. 39, pt. 1, 251-252. The Confederates treated the men detailed as nurses as such, and when their services were no longer needed, they were permitted to travel to Vicksburg. Reed, *The 12th Iowa*, 158-159.

the previous day by the Confederates. Coon's brigade took position on the army's left covering the Verona road.[2]

Advancing beyond the ruins of Harrisburg, Winslow's troopers clashed with and drove in pickets from the 14th Confederate. Winslow deployed the 3d Iowa and pressed to within sight of the Rebel breastworks at Mrs. Sample's, which were held by Mabry's brigade and Lyon's dismounted division. After skirmishing for about two hours, Winslow, in obedience to orders from Grierson, recalled his horsesoldiers and retired into the lines held by Smith's infantry.[3] Shortly thereafter, word was received that the Confederates were threatening the Union left, and Winslow rode to the southeast and reinforced Coon's brigade.[4]

Meanwhile, Smith had alerted his infantry commanders to have their troops and trains ready to move. Colonel Moore's division would take the lead. About noon, the Confederates having made no demonstration, Smith sent Moore orders to withdraw his troops, march into Tupelo, and turn his column into the Ellistown road. The division was to proceed "very slowly, the train to follow with sick and wounded, protected well on the flanks by a brigade of cavalry and in the rear by the colored brigade."[5] Except for suffering caused by the excessive heat, the Third Division's afternoon march from the battlefield, through Tupelo, and out the Ellistown road was uneventful. The troops, after crossing Oldtown Creek on a "rickety old bridge," halted and camped on the ridge beyond. Some of the soldiers of Gilbert's brigade located a mill along the stream, in which there was

2 *O.R.*, Series I, Vol. 39, pt. 1, 251, 304, 306, 316, 317. When Coon's troopers took the field, the 2d Iowa was on the left and the 9th Illinois on the right.

3 Ibid., 306, 310, 312, 314; Scott, *Story of a Cavalry Regiment*, 289.

4 *O.R.*, Series I, Vol. 39, pt. 1, 310, 314.

5 Ibid., 253.

some freshly ground corn. This they took with them and the messes were soon busy preparing "hasty pudding."[6]

Prior to the withdrawal of the Third Division, Mower redeployed his brigades. Woods's brigade was shifted to the left—the 12th and 35th Iowa occupied the ground south of the Pontotoc road defended by Murray's troops on the previous day. The 33d Missouri and the 7th Minnesota relieved those two regiments, while Ward's brigade extended to the left to occupy the breastworks erected by the 35th Iowa and the right battalion of the 33d Missouri. McClure's and McMillen's brigades were tapped for duty as a ready reserve.[7]

Both Generals Lee and Forrest believed in attack, and, despite the drubbing four of their brigades had taken in the battle of Tupelo on the 14th, they had their troops in motion early the next morning, as they probed for a weak point in the foe's position. Chalmers, as soon as Winslow's bluecoats started to pull back, ordered McCulloch's brigade into the saddle. Reaching the ridge overlooking Harrisburg Branch, the Rebels saw that the Union infantry was still on the field. Chalmers then moved toward the northeast to see if he could pinpoint Smith's right flank. Brushing aside Union patrols, Chalmers was able to gain a position from where he could see the Ellistown road, and he observed Moore's column en route to Oldtown Creek. Accompanied by McCulloch's people, Chalmers rejoined General Lee on the Pontotoc road and reported what he had seen.[8]

General Lee, in the meantime, had voiced fears that the foe, emboldened by his victory of yesterday, would strike southward, and lay waste the ripening crops of the Black Prairie Region. He had accordingly massed most of Forrest's corps, except for the units holding the breastworks at

6 Ibid., 281, 287, 290, 292, 293; Scott, *Story of the 32d Iowa*, 293.

7 *O.R.*, Series I, Vol. 39, pt. 1, 259, 266, 269, 270, 271, 273, 275, 277.

8 Ibid., 327.

Mrs. Sample's, across the Tupelo-Verona road, three miles north of the latter point. There being no indication that the Yankees planned to exploit their success, General Forrest ordered Buford to advance up the Verona road and assail Smith's left. Buford moved forward, and, when within two and one-half miles of Tupelo, he dismounted and deployed his three brigades—Bell to the left, Crossland in the center, and Rucker on the right.[9]

About the hour that Buford left Calhoun's, Colonel Bouton, whose brigade was to follow the Third Division and guard the train, had recalled his troops and formed them in the hollow where the supply wagons were corralled. The line formerly held by his brigade and Gilbert's was now the responsibility of the cavalry.

The wagons, Battery I, and the 59th U.S. Colored Troops had moved out, and the 61st had just fallen in, when Buford's people assailed the line of outposts defended by Grierson's horsesoldiers. While Forrest watched, Buford's three brigades bore back, for a least a mile, the picket line manned by the 9th Illinois and 10th Missouri Cavalry, reinforced by skirmishers of the 93d Indiana.

General Mower, who was supervising the Union withdrawal, sent word for Bouton to recall the 61st U.S.C.T. and hold it and the 68th ready "to meet any movements of the enemy." Colonel McClure occupied with his brigade the breastworks to the left of Woods's people. To cover his left and establish contact with the cavalry, McClure deployed the 9th Minnesota to his left and rear. One section of the 2d Iowa Battery came pounding up, and the redlegs put their guns into battery along McClure's left, and in support of Cram's section of Battery E, 1st Illinois Light Artillery. Thus, by the time Buford's skirmishers had gained the ridge

9 Ibid., 323, 331, 337, 343; Hancock, *Diary*, 431; Lee, "Battle of Tupelo," *Publications*, Vol. 6, 48-49. Crossland's brigade was to the west of the Verona road and Rucker's to the east.

held by Bouton on the 14th, the Federals had massed a formidable force to meet his thrust.[10]

Colonel Bouton had formed the 61st and the 68th U.S.C.T. in line of battle. Advancing through a belt of timber, the blacks, on emerging from its southern verge, sighted Buford's division. Bouton called for his Negroes to charge the Rebels with bayonets. The 61st U.S.C.T. and a battalion of the 68th let go a shout for the Union, and surged forward. The black brigade was supported on the left by the 9th Illinois Cavalry and on the right by the 9th Minnesota of McClure's brigade and the 97th Indiana of McMillen's. The cannoneers of sections of the 2d Iowa and Battery E hammered Buford's line with shell. The heat, which was oppressive, had felled a number of the Confederates as they drove back the cavalry. Buford recalled that at least 80 men were carried to the rear with heat exhaustion. The skirmishers, screening Buford's battle line, were driven from their position on the ridge. Bouton's soldiers followed them about 800 yards, but the pursuit was called off before contact was established with Buford's battle line. The Federals, having cleared the sector to their immediate front, retired to a ridge near the timber.[11]

Meanwhile, General Lyon had advanced his dismounted division spearheaded by skirmishers of the 14th Confederate, to probe the Union defenses flanking the Pontotoc road. The Confederates debouched from the woods, crossed Harrisburg Branch, and cautiously felt their way up the opposite slope. Mower, hoping to punish the Rebels, cautioned Woods and Ward to have their men stay concealed behind the breastworks until the foe approached within 50 yards. Lyon sensed a trap, however. He halted his troops about 200

10 Hancock, *Diary*, 431; *O.R.*, Series I, Vol. 39, pt. 1, 253, 258, 259, 262, 266, 267, 278, 303, 314, 317, 323; Cowden, *History of the 59th U.S.C.T.*, 130.

11 *O.R.*, Series I, Vol. 39, pt. 1, 253, 262-263, 267, 303, 317, 323, 331-332, 337, 345, 347-348.

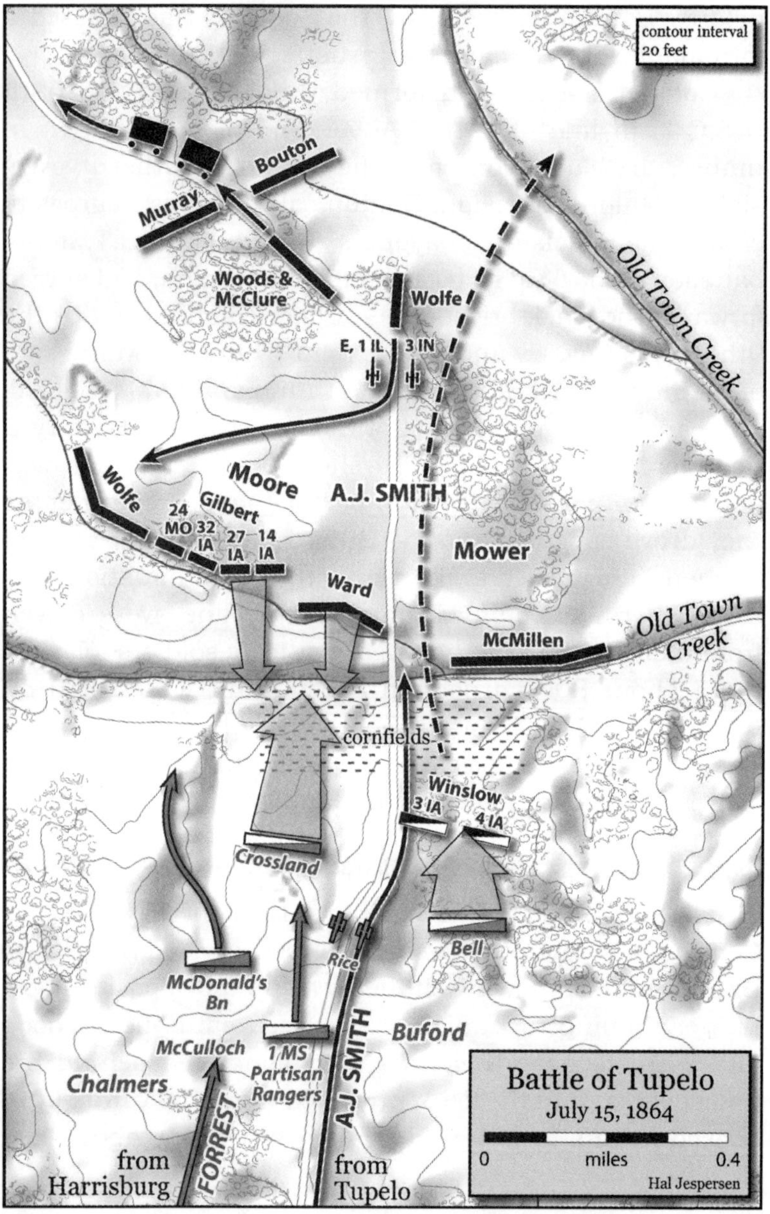
contour interval
20 feet
Bouton
Murray
Woods &
McClure
Wolfe
E, 1 IL
3 IN
Old Town Creek
Wolfe
Moore
A.J. SMITH
Gilbert
24
MO
32
IA
27
IA
14
IA
Mower
Ward
Old Town
Creek
McMillen
cornfields
Winslow
3 IA
4 IA
Crossland
Bell
Rice
McDonald's
Bn
Buford
McCulloch
1 MS
Partisan
Rangers
Chalmers
A.J. SMITH
FORREST
from
Harrisburg
from
Tupelo
Battle of Tupelo
July 15, 1864
0
miles
0.4
Hal Jespersen

The Confederates initially caught the Federals off-guard while they were going into camp at Oldtown Creek and drove back the enemy cavalry in some confusion. The heat, the excessive losses suffered on the 14th, and a quick infantry response, however, ended the fight in favor of the Federals.

---

yards away, where they took cover and opened fire. The Federals, who had previously fixed bayonets, lay down until it became apparent that the butternuts were not going to come any closer. Mower now ordered a charge, and Woods's men leaped to their feet, vaulted the barricades, and raced toward the foe. Lyon's people and the 14th Confederate took to their heels. With their head start, the Rebels were able to outdistance Woods's panting soldiers. After pursuing the foe about one-half mile, Woods called a halt. Each regiment in the brigade then deployed two companies as skirmishers, and Woods, having cleared the area to his immediate front, marched his troops back past the ruins of Harrisburg.[12]

The Confederates who had been threatening his left and center having been repulsed, Mower now assembled

12 Ibid., 258, 269, 270, 271, 275, 350, 351; Reed, *The 12th Iowa*, 160. In this action, Woods's brigade lost four killed and 31 wounded, besides a number of men felled by sunstroke. | | Newly promoted Brig. Gen. Harlan B. Hylan, who's commission dated only from June 14, 1864, played little role in the Tupelo Campaign. This was unusual, for he was in the thick of things at Brice's Crossroads; and was endorsed by Forrest for his skill and bravery in that fight. Lyon was also a West Pointer, class of 1856, with pre-war regular army service out west. He began the war as an infantryman and was captured at Fort Donelson. In 1863, Joseph Johnston assigned him an ad-hoc cavalry command outside of Vicksburg, he later requested to be transferred to that branch. He was assigned to Wheeler's cavalry corps later that summer and served with the Army of Tennessee up through the defeat at Missionary Ridge and the subsequent retreat to Dalton, Georgia, where he was credited with saving much of the army's surviving artillery. Described as one of Forrest's most ardent supporters, the decision to transfer Lyon to a scratch infantry division during the Tupelo campaign was all the more curious since Lyon's command had so little chance to get into action. Brian Steel Wills, "Brig. Gen. Hylan Benton Lyon," *Kentuckians in Gray*, 180-186.

his division and moved out to overtake the Third Division. Bouton's brigade preceded Mower's division, while Winslow's horsesoldiers, reinforced by the 9th Illinois Cavalry, screened the column's rear as it passed through Tupelo and tramped northwestward up the Ellistown road. General Grierson, as it was the place of danger, rode with the rear guard.[13]

As soon as General Forrest learned that Chalmers had sighted an enemy column marching up the Ellistown road toward Oldtown Creek, he concluded, correctly, that A. J. Smith had had enough and was retiring on the railhead at La Grange. Calling for Roddey, Forrest rode for Harrisburg. He reached there just as the cavalry, which was screening Mower's rear, was moving out. Roddey's lead regiment, the 5th Alabama Cavalry, was thrown forward, but it was unable to stampede the 9th Illinois. General Buford now came up with Crossland's and Bell's brigades, and Rice's Battery, and he was ordered by Forrest "to press forward in the direction of Tupelo, and engage the enemy there, if he still occupied the place." Meanwhile, General Lee had placed Forrest in charge of the pursuit. Forrest now ordered Mabry's brigade to establish a roadblock on the Chesterville road. Chalmers was to follow Buford with McCulloch's brigade.[14]

Forrest instructed Buford and Chalmers to turn their columns into the Harrisburg-Ellistown road, which intersected the route along which the Federals were marching, one mile south of Oldtown Creek. Forrest and Lee then rode into Tupelo. There they found several of the houses burned, and the rest turned into field hospitals. The wounded, Yank and Reb, were tended by men detailed for

13 *O.R.*, Series I, Vol. 39, pt. 1, 258, 259, 304, 306, 310, 312, 314, 316, 317, 319. When Mower's division moved out, McMillen's brigade was the last infantry unit to leave the battlefield. The 7th Kansas Cavalry had marched with the Third Division, serving as the army's vanguard.

14 Ibid., 323, 327, 332, 337, 348, 350; Hancock, *Diary*, 43-432; Lee, "Battle of Tupelo," *Publications*, Vol. 6, 48-49; *History of the 9th Illinois Cavalry*, 121-122.

that purpose by A. J. Smith's brigade commanders. Even so, the wounds of many of the men were already fly-blown and filled with maggots.

After Generals Lee and Forrest had canvassed the situation, Forrest, accompanied by his escort, started up the Ellistown road. Three miles from Tupelo, he "heard heavy artillery firing "to his front. The general touched his spurs to his horse's flank and the gait quickened. As he approached Oldtown Creek, he saw that Buford and Chalmers had overtaken the foe and were hotly engaged.[15]

When the lead brigade of Mower's division reached Oldtown Creek, hard on the heels of Bouton's brigade, it was ordered to cross the stream, pass beyond the camps of the Third Division, and take position in front. It would then be prepared to take the advance in the morning. Just as the rear brigade, McMillen's, had crossed the stream, Buford's column attacked the Union cavalry.

General Grierson had not been informed of A. J. Smith's plan to spend the night of July 15 on Oldtown Creek, so he was surprised when he came down into the bottom and found the train corralled. This was unfortunate for the Federals, because Buford's division was able to occupy ground commanding the bottom and the crossing. Rice's cannoneers threw their four 6-pounders into battery and shelled the corral and crossing, while Crossland's and Bell's brigades were dismounted and formed into line of battle—Bell's to the right of the road and Crossland's to the left.[16]

15 *O.R.*, Series I, Vol. 39, pt. 1, 323; Wyeth, *Life of General N. B. Forrest*, 454; Hancock, *Diary*, 432.

16 *O.R.*, Series I, Vol. 39, pt. 1, 253, 305, 337, 340, 343, 348; Hancock, *Diary*, 432, The two brigades with Buford numbered about 1,000 effectives. Bell's brigade had the lead as Buford's division advanced up the road from Harrisburg. From left to right Bell's brigade was deployed; the 2d, 15th, 16th, and Newsom's regiments.

COL. TYREE H. BELL

A Tennessee planter, Bell commanded the brigade that spearheaded the attack at Old Town Creek.

Library of Congress

Spearheaded by the 16th Tennessee, the Rebels charged the Union cavalry. Winslow quickly dismounted and deployed the 3d and 4th Iowa to receive Bell's charge. General Smith, seeing that the horsesoldiers were in trouble, called on Mower and Moore for help. Mower shouted for McMillen to recross Oldtown Creek, while Colonel Moore ordered first Gilbert's brigade and then Wolfe's to Winslow's assistance.

If the Confederates had attacked in greater strength, the Federals might have been in serious trouble, for as McMillen countermarched his people across Oldtown Creek, he was delayed by Union cavalry falling back in confusion. Troopers of the 4th Iowa were heard to cry in despair that "they did not fight on foot." Once on the south side of the stream, McMillen placed his soldiers to the right of the road, as the cannoneers of Battery E unlimbered their two guns.[17] Gilbert, upon receipt of orders to march to the cavalry's support, turned out his brigade and deployed it to the right of the 33d Wisconsin. The regimental historian of the 32d Iowa recalled that at the moment Rice's guns roared into action Maj. Jonathan

17 *O.R.*, Series I, Vol. 39, pt. 1, 253, 258, 260, 261, 263, 264. From left to right McMillen deployed his brigade: the 114th Illinois, the 93d Indiana, and the 95th and 72d Ohio. The 10th Minnesota did not re-cross Oldtown Creek in time to participate in the engagement.

Hutchinson and Adj. W. L. Carpenter had tied their horses to a small tree just behind the gun stacks. A shell struck the tree, and, exploding, one fragment just missed one of the Iowans. Major Hutchinson called, "Thirty-second into line! Quick! Quick!" The brigade, on forming, found itself in a cornfield south of the road. Only two of Gilbert's regiments, the 14th and 27th Iowa, were in position, when he was told to recross Oldtown Creek. Covered by a strong skirmish line, Gilbert's people moved out on the double, supported on the right by two dismounted battalions of the 9th Illinois Cavalry. A fence was climbed, a waist-deep stream was waded, an underbrush-choked island crossed, and a second channel forded. Pushing on, Gilbert's brigade passed through a skirt of woods and entered a large cornfield. On the opposite side was a "rebel line, which with its battle-flags waving in the sunlight, was boldly and firmly advancing."[18]

Gilbert's brigade on reaching the cornfield was deployed from right to left: the 32d, 14th, and 27th Iowa. The 24th Missouri became separated from the brigade on crossing Oldtown Creek and did not participate in the engagement. As soon as Gilbert's brigade had taken position west of the road, McMillen prepared to assail the Rebels to his front.

Although Crossland and Bell had been able to deploy only 1,000 men between them, Buford's spirits soared as he watched them roll back Grierson's horsesoldiers. With his glasses he could see that Rice's artillerists had thrown the wagon corral, on the far side of the creek, into confusion. Many of the teamsters had panicked. Union resistance stiffened as McMillen's and Gilbert's infantry recrossed Oldtown Creek and entered the fight. On the left, as his brigade moved against Gilbert's battle line, Crossland was wounded and compelled to retire from the field. Command of the Kentucky Brigade devolved on Lt.

18 Ibid., 281, 287, 290, 292, 293; Scott, *Story of the 32d Iowa*, 293.

Col. A. R. Shacklett of the 8th Kentucky Mounted Infantry. Casualties among the Confederates were heavy, as they advanced on and were repulsed by Union footsoldiers, supported by dismounted troops of the 3d and 4th Iowa Cavalry and 9th Illinois Cavalry.

Seizing the initiative, the bluecoats counter-attacked and beat back the foe. Buford was preparing to abandon his position on the ridge overlooking Oldtown Creek, when Chalmers rode up at the head of McCulloch's brigade. In an effort to stabilize the situation, Chalmers committed each regiment as it trotted up, rather than sending in the entire brigade. This was poor tactics and Chalmers knew it. As to be expected, each unit in turn was repulsed and beaten back in confusion.[19]

General Forrest now galloped up and told Chalmers to employ McCulloch's brigade in support of Rice's battery. Chalmers placed himself at the head of Forrest's Alabama Cavalry Regiment and rode to the left to oppose Gilbert's surge. General Forrest followed, and as he did he received a painful wound in the right big toe, which incapacitated him. An aide was sent to tell Chalmers to take charge and withdraw the troops, while a staff officer headed for Tupelo to advise General Lee of what had happened.[20]

Chalmers assumed command at a most inauspicious moment. The tide had turned, and along the entire front his people were being hard-pressed. Colonel McCulloch was cut down, with a wound in the shoulder. Orders were now issued by Chalmers for Buford to re-form his division.

19 || Thomas Parson attributes this piecemeal commitment to Forrest, not Chalmers. "Forrest directed Chalmers to feed his regiments into the fight on the left as they arrived. . . . Chalmers admitted, 'consequently, the advanced regiments were driven back in confusion before the rear could be engaged.'" Parson, *Work for Giants*, 254.

20 *O.R.*, Series I, Vol. 39, pt, 1, 323-324, 327, 332, 337, 340, 341, 343-344, 348; Hancock, *Diary*, 432-433; Lee, "Battle of Tupelo," *Publications*, Vol. 6, 49.

COL. ROBERT "BLACK BOB" McCULLOCH

McCulloch, of the 2nd Missouri Cavalry, CSA.

Wyeth, *Life of Lieutenant General Nathan Bedford Forrest*

He received an answer that it was impossible. This order was repeated, and Chalmers was told that Buford had rallied three companies. There was nothing he could do but withdraw Rice's Battery and abandon the ridge overlooking Oldtown Creek. McCulloch's troopers were remounted and screened the retreat, after which a roadblock was established about 400 yards to the rear.[21]

The torrid weather and the Confederates felled a number of Federals as they advanced and occupied the ridge. Union plans did not call for a resumption of the offensive, so Gilbert and McMillen halted their battle lines and pushed forward skirmishers on dislodging the Rebels. Mower's division was to have the lead on the 16th, consequently, McMillen's brigade was recalled. It was replaced south of the stream by Wolfe's brigade of Moore's division. On crossing Oldtown Creek, Wolfe posted his brigade on Gilbert's right. Gilbert, on the recall of McMillen and prior to Wolfe's arrival, had shifted his brigade to the left, anchoring its right flank on

21 *O.R.*, Series I, Vol. 39, pt. 1, 327, 332.

the Ellistown road.[22] The cavalry, like McMillen, crossed Oldtown Creek and bivouacked.[23]

When the Federals failed to exploit their success, Chalmers ordered McCulloch's brigade to return to its camp at Mrs. Sample's, while he went in search of General Lee. He found Lee, who was determined to hold the ground, striving to re-form Buford's division. Buford was told to deploy his brigades to the left and right of the Ellistown road and be ready to harass the foe in the morning. Buford, however, was unable to collect sufficient men to discharge this mission, and McCulloch's brigade had to be recalled. Buford's troopers then rode back to their camp, on a small stream two miles from the scene of the fight.[24]

In the Confederate camps there were rumors that Forrest had been killed. As to be expected, this caused much apprehension. This was reported to Forrest, who had been taken to a Tupelo field hospital, where the hemorrhage was arrested and the wound dressed. To disprove the rumor, he mounted his horse, and "without even taking time to put on his coat, rode in his shirt-sleeves at a gallop along the line of troopers, cheering them not only by his presence, but with encouraging words, assuring them that it was only a slight flesh wound, and he was still able and ready to lead them." One of the soldiers recalled, "The effect produced upon the men by the appearance of General Forrest is indescribable. They seem wild with joy at seeing their great leader still with them."[25]

22 Ibid., 258, 260, 263, 287, 296. In gaining this ridge, Gilbert's troops had fought their way across a large cornfield, up a grade, across a fence, and through "the broken timber to the crest of the hill." Ibid., 287.

23 Ibid., 306, 311, 314, 316, 318; Scott, *Story of a Cavalry Regiment*, 290.

24 *O.R.*, Series I, Vol. 39, pt. 1, 327-328, 332, 344; Hancock, *Diary*, 433; Lee, "Battle of Tupelo," *Publications*, Vol. 6, 49-50

25 Wyeth, *Life of General N. B. Forrest*, 454-455.

Captain Tyler and his men, during the day, had continued to operate east of Tupelo. At 3 p.m. Tyler learned from his scouts that Smith's columns were retreating via the Ellistown road. In hopes of delaying the Federals, Tyler assembled his combat patrol, and, swinging well to the east of Oldtown Creek, establish a roadblock at the Yonaba Creek bridge.[26]

General Smith had his army on the road by sun-up. Mower's division on July 16 had the lead. Despite their proximity to Rebel outposts, Wolfe and Gilbert experienced no difficulty in withdrawing across Oldtown Creek, where they rejoined the Third Division. Winslow's mounted brigade, reinforced by the 7th Kansas Cavalry, shielded the rear of the column as it marched along under a hot Mississippi sun. Since there was a good supply of water available, A. J. Smith determined to halt and spend the night at Ellistown. Most of the troops had fallen out and started preparing their evening rations, when the boom of a cannon was heard.[27]

As the horses and men were exhausted, while the frightful casualties of the 14th had sapped the corps' effectiveness, General Lee determined not to follow the foe any farther in force. General Chalmers was directed to pursue and harass the retreating Federals with Roddey's division and Rucker's brigade. The Confederate vanguard soon came up with the 7th Kansas Cavalry, which was screening the rear of Smith's column. The Rebels, having been badly hurt in the fighting of the three previous days, did not press the bluecoats hard and only a few shots, at extreme ranges, were exchanged. When Smith halted at Ellistown, Company A, 3d Iowa Cavalry, was assigned to picket the Tupelo road. Soon after the Iowans took position, the butternuts became bolder, and the officer in charge of the outposts called for help. Grierson turned out the 7th

26 *O.R.*, Series I, Vol. 39, pt. 1, 345.

27 Ibid., 253, 294, 296, 303, 306, 311, 314, 316, 319; Scott, *Story of the 32d Iowa*, 294.

Kansas Cavalry, and Colonel Moore counter-marched Wolfe's brigade and Battery G's guns. The redlegs unlimbered their guns, and fired a few rounds, while the horsesoldiers pressed the Confederates. Seeing that he was badly outnumbered, Chalmers recalled his vanguard and camped.[28]

Chalmers, assuming that the Yanks would cross the Tallahatchie at Kelly's Mill, now ordered Roddey's division to intercept them there. He would follow with Rucker's brigade and harass Smith's rearguard. A. J. Smith was cagey. On the 17th he turned his columns into the New Albany road and crossed the Tallahatchie at New Albany, rather than at Kelly's Mill, where Roddey was waiting. During the morning's march, Rucker's people clashed on several occasions with the Union rearguard, Coon's brigade. Chalmers by noon saw that he had been hoodwinked. He therefore called off the pursuit and returned to Harrisburg with Rucker's brigade. An aide was sent galloping to tell Roddey that the foe had given them the slip, and with orders for him to recall his division and march to Tupelo. Captain Tyler and his combat patrol had also failed to establish contact with the bluecoats.[29]

The Federals spent the night of July 17 in and around New Albany, with Winslow's brigade camped four miles northwest of town on the Holly Springs road. On the 18th Smith marched to Vaughan's Ford on Tippah River, and

28 *O.R.*, Series I, Vol. 39, pt. 1, 296, 306, 311, 319, 328; Scott, *Story of a Cavalry Regiment*, 290; Scott, *Story of the 32d Iowa*, 294; Hancock, *Diary*, 433-434. When the artillery went into action, Smith's infantry commanders called out their men and formed them into line of battle. Here they stood until Chalmers retired.

29 *O.R.*, Series I, Vol. 39, pt. 1, 253, 328, 345; Young, *The 7th Tennessee Cavalry*, 99-100. On the 16th Tyler had discovered that the Federals were on the Ellistown road, so he had abandoned his roadblock at the crossing of the Yonaba and had taken position on the Ellistown-Ripley road. When he learned on the 17th that the Federals were en route for New Albany, he took cognizance of the jaded condition of the horses and returned to Harrisburg.

encamped. The next evening found him at Salem, and on July 20 the advance reached La Grange about noon. Mower's and Moore's infantry divisions halted at Davis's Mill. The footsoldiers marched to the railhead the next day.[30]

The return march in the terrible heat, along dusty roads, with the soldiers on half-rations, and water scarce was a trying ordeal that tested the soldiers' zeal and patriotism. Many of the horses broke down, and Grierson's troopers spent as much time in search of forage as they did scouting and patrolling. At Salem on the evening of the 19th, the Yanks were delighted to find a supply train sent by General Hatch which alleviated much of the suffering.[31]

Smith now broke up his force. The infantry was "given another free ride on box cars into Memphis," and by nightfall on July 23 the soldiers were back in the camps they had occupied prior to the Tupelo Campaign. Grierson's horsesoldiers and the train returned to Memphis by way of the State Line Road.[32]

Like most Civil War operations, the Tupelo Campaign did not result in the destruction of either contending army. This enabled the veterans of the campaign and the arm chair generals of the twentieth century to argue as to the ultimate victor. The Confederates admitted, while they had suffered a bloody repulse on the morning of July 14, General A. J. Smith had abandoned the field the next day. This, they claimed, showed that Smith "in being so remote from succor" and his base of supplies, did not "feel the sense of security which usually belongs to the victor."

30 *O.R.*, Series I, Vol. 39, pt. 1, 253, 303, 306, 316.

31 Ibid., 253; Scott, *Story of a Cavalry Regiment*, 290-291; Scott, *Story of the 32d Iowa*, 294; Cowden, *History of the 59th U.S.C.T.*, 130; Bryner, *Bugle Echoes*, 133.

32 Reed, *The 12th Iowa*, 166; Scott, *Story of the 32d Iowa*, 294; Bryner, *Bugle Echoes*, 134.

Forrest's friends and biographers have held that even if the battle at Harrisburg on the 14th was a victory for A. J. Smith, it could not in fairness be considered a defeat of Forrest.

The author cannot agree with the conclusions advanced by Forrest's biographers and many of today's historians that the Tupelo Campaign was a stand-off and of no significance. We must recall that A. J. Smith's mission was to keep Forrest's corps from wrecking the single track railroad over which General Sherman supplied his "Army Group" in northwest Georgia, and to destroy Forrest's command as an effective combat unit. He would also have to move cautiously to keep Forrest from turning the tables on him, as he had on Sooy Smith in February and Sturgis in June. Smith accordingly advanced with his army well-closed up and prepared to deploy on short notice.

General Lee, stung by the amphibious thrust into Jefferson and Claiborne counties, Slocum's advance to Jackson, and the threat to Mobile, was unable to concentrate his maximum available force against A. J. Smith. Because of vigorous opposition by the governors of Mississippi and Alabama, it was impossible for Lee to abandon additional territory to increase further Forrest's striking force. Moreover, the pressure exerted on these points compelled Lee to abandon the plan to let the Federals attack Forrest's corps in a fortified position near Okolona, and take advantage of the anticipated repulse to seize the initiative. The confusion brought about by the unexpected change in plans enabled A. J. Smith on the 13th to steal a march on Forrest. Smith took advantage of this situation to occupy a strong position, of his choosing, on the ridge east of Harrisburg. The pressure exerted by Slocum and the threat to Mobile forced General Lee's hand and he ordered an attack. In the fight on the 14th, four of Forrest's seven mounted brigades were so terribly mauled that their combat effectiveness was destroyed.

A. J. Smith now became overly cautious. He failed to follow up the Confederate repulse with a savage counterattack, which might have annihilated Forrest's corps. Once before, at Champion Hill on May 16, 1863, he had failed to attack, when the opportunity was ripe and the chance for destroying Lt. Gen. John C. Pemberton's army had presented itself.[33]

On July 15 the Federals, their supplies running short, abandoned their position at Harrisburg and started for Memphis. The Confederates pursued, overtook Smith's rearguard at Oldtown Creek, and suffered a repulse. A conversation that took place that evening illustrates the condition of at least one of Forrest's divisions at that time:

> *General Forrest*: "General Buford, move your division."
>
> *General Buford*: "I have no division, General Forrest."
>
> *G. F.*: "Where is your division?"
>
> *G. B.*: "They are dead and wounded."[34]

To the critical observer, it is apparent that A. J. Smith and to a lesser extent Sturgis accomplished their missions. Forrest's corps, the one cavalry force Sherman feared, was kept in northeast Mississippi in June and July and off the railroad over which his "Army Group" was supplied. If the railroad had been cut and put out of action for a week, or ten days, during this period it would have been disastrous for the Union. The combat effectiveness of Forrest's corps was destroyed in the period of July 13-15. While Forrest would rally his force and make a number of daring raids, never again would his corps be able to stand and fight

33 || Historian Timothy B. Smith, in his study of Champion Hill, attributes much of Smith's caution at that battle to his corps commander, John McClernand, and to Ulysses S. Grant. Timothy B. Smith, *Champion Hill, Decisive Battle for Vicksburg* (New York: 2004), 342.

34 Hancock, *Diary*, 435.

Union infantry. General Sherman, however, did not realize this at the time, so he ordered A. J. Smith, on his return to Memphis, to make another attempt to get Forrest.

The body count has always been important in wars in which western nations are involved. On returning to Memphis, A. J. Smith listed his casualties in the campaign as: 77 killed, 559 wounded, and 38 captured. He reported 3,000 Confederate casualties, 1,800 on July 14. General Forrest announced his losses as 210 killed and 1,116 wounded. No mention was made of captured or missing.[35]

35 *O.R.*, Series I, Vol. 39, pt. 1, 252, 256, 324.

6

General Slocum Goes to Jackson

GENERAL Washburn knew that Maj. Gen. Edward R. S. Canby, the commander of the Union forces operating in Louisiana, would be interested in Sturgis's Brice's Crossroads debacle. Meanwhile, word had reached Memphis from Canby's New Orleans headquarters that it was feared the Trans-Mississippi Confederates were massing columns to send against the blueclad forces of Maj. Gen. Frederick Steele guarding the approaches to Little Rock and Pine Bluff, Arkansas. This information, coupled with Sturgis's rout, caused Washburn to question the wisdom of orders alerting A. J. Smith and his troops to hold themselves ready to proceed to New Orleans, to join the array Canby was massing to attack Mobile. Washburn accordingly on June 12, 1864, forwarded a dispatch to Canby's headquarters, telling of Sturgis's defeat.[1]

It took the steamboat with Washburn's message four days to make the run from Memphis to New Orleans. After studying his maps and discussing the situation with his staff, General Canby on the 16th determined to apply pressure on the Mississippi Confederates to keep the "Devil Forrest" pinned down and prevent him from striking at the

1 *O.R.*, Series I, Vol. 39, pt. 2, 107. General Canby was in charge of the Military Division of West Mississippi, which included the Departments of the Gulf and of Arkansas. General Steele commanded the Department of Arkansas.

railroads over which General Sherman's "Army Group" received its supplies and reinforcements. Orders were drafted for Maj. Gen. Henry W. Slocum, the commander at Vicksburg, to hold 2,000 footsoldiers ready for service in the field. This force was to be prepared to move to New Orleans to join the army Canby was organizing to send against Mobile. All cavalry was to be ready for "a rapid movement into the interior of the State." This thrust was to be made in "concert with other operations, and the time, route, and object of the movement" was to be determined by Canby.[2] Washburn was notified of these plans.[3]

On June 20, six days before he learned of Canby's plans, General Washburn wrote the New Orleans commander, detailing his plans to send A. J. Smith with 9,000 infantry and 3,000 cavalry to maul Forrest. It would be a number of days, he cautioned, before the build-up at La Grange would be completed and Smith able to leave the railroad. By then, the wily Forrest would have learned from his scouts of what was afoot. Reports had reached Memphis, which subsequently proved unfounded, that Forrest was concentrating his corps north of Grenada.

Washburn, although he was junior to Canby, suggested that Canby might be able to capture Mobile, while A. J.

2 Ibid., 126. General Slocum had assumed command of the District of Vicksburg on May 6, 1864. || Henry Slocum had come to Mississippi in unusual circumstances. He was formerly the commander of the XII Corps, Army of the Potomac, until his command and the XI Corps were transferred west to help save Chattanooga in the fall of 1863. At that time Slocum was placed under the command of Mag. Gen. Joseph Hooker, who had formerly commanded the Army of the Potomac at the battle of Chancellorsville. Slocum blamed Hooker for that defeat and refused to continue to serve under him, going so far as to complain to Abraham Lincoln. Lincoln dumped the problem onto Maj. Gen. William S. Rosecrans, and after Rosecrans was replaced, onto Ulysses S. Grant. Grant's solution was to transfer Slocum to Mississippi. David A. Powell, *The Impulse of Victory, Ulysses S. Grant at Chattanooga* (Carbondale, IL: 2020), 38-39.

3 Ibid., 125. Washburn did not learn of Canby's actions until June 26.

Smith kept Forrest occupied in northern Mississippi. Ten thousand troops from New Orleans, if they moved promptly, could make an amphibious landing at Pascagoula, and pressing on seize Mobile, before the Rebels could concentrate in sufficient force to oppose the thrust.[4]

Meanwhile, General Slocum at Vicksburg had received Canby's order to hold 2,000 infantry ready for immediate service. On June 22, Slocum contacted Brig. Gen. John P. Hawkins, the commander of the 1st Colored Division. Hawkins was told to hold a force of that number in readiness. "The time and object of the expedition" would be made known to him, as soon as Slocum and Washburn had coordinated their plans for a joint operation.[5]

One of the great problems confronting Civil War officers was communications. On June 27 Washburn telegraphed General Sherman, complaining that Slocum had failed to acknowledge a request made ten days before. According to Washburn, he had asked Slocum to send a column from Vicksburg "to make a diversion in favor of A. J. Smith, and break up the Mississippi Central Railroad."[6] Now, Washburn continued, orders had been issued to Col. Joseph Karge to embark his cavalry brigade on boats and to proceed from Memphis to Vicksburg. After going ashore at the "Hill City," Karge's column was to make a dash for the Mobile & Ohio Railroad, and, if possible, wreck it from Macon to Meridian. The Union troopers also were to cut the Mississippi Central Railroad. Karge would ask Slocum to reinforce his brigade before it left Vicksburg. Washburn theorized that if Karge were successful, Forrest would be

4 Ibid., 131.

5 Ibid., 140. Two of Hawkins's four brigades were camped in and around Vicksburg. Ibid., 69.

6 An examination of the Official Records and documents on file at the National Archives has failed to turn up a copy of the dispatch to which Washburn refers.

MAJ. GEN. HENRY W. SLOCUM

Slocum led the Union XII Corps at Gettysburg and went on to serve as district commander at Vicksburg in 1864.

Library of Congress

unable to rush troops to the defense of Mobile or to supply his corps through Meridian.[7]

Unknown to Washburn, General Canby on June 27 was writing General Sherman of the steps he had taken to insure Forrest's downfall. Orders had been issued placing under Washburn's control the militia units from the states of the "Old Northwest" previously alerted to report to Canby, along with several regiments of veteran-volunteers from Missouri. The addition of these units would provide A. J. Smith with from 12,000 to 15,000 effectives,

7 Ibid., 148-149. | | Joseph Karge was a former Prussian officer of Polish birth. He was also a fervent Polish nationalist and liberal revolutionary. Born in 1823, in Posen (Poznan) he was educated at the University of Breslau and in Paris. Drafted into the Prussian army in 1846, he deserted his regiment, the Royal Horse Guards stationed in Berlin, when revolts broke out in 1848. He emigrated to America in 1851. In 1861, he helped organize the 1st New Jersey Cavalry, serving in Virginia for the next two years. While recuperating from a leg wound suffered in 1862, he helped recruit and organize the 2nd New Jersey Cavalry, which was assigned to the Western Theater. Karge was an excellent regimental and brigade commander. He proved an able rear-guard commander at the fiasco of Brice's Crossroads. See Joseph Wroblewski, "New Jersey's Uhlan, Brevet Brigadier General Joseph Karge," *Garden State Legacy*, no. 50, (December, 2020). Online edition found at https://gardenstatelegacy.com/files/New_Jerseys_Uhlan_Wroblewski_GSL50.pdf; and Francis C. Kajencki, *Star on Many a Battlefield: Brevet Brigadier General Joseph Karge in the American Civil War* (Rutherford, NJ: Farleigh Dickenson University Press, 1980).

and still permit Washburn to maintain a mobile reserve of 5,000 in the Memphis area. Cavalry columns were to drive inland from Vicksburg and Baton Rouge with the object of "distracting the attention of the enemy from Smith's operations." A powerful amphibious force was being outfitted at New Orleans to move against Mobile, in conjunction with A. J. Smith's thrust and the cavalry raids.[8]

Slocum on June 28 was overwhelmed by the receipt of letters from three ranking generals, all urging him to take the offensive. The fiery Sherman had read in an Atlanta paper of the 25th (there was no censorship and newspapers passed readily through the lines; Sherman, like most of the successful Civil War generals, obtained much valuable military information from enemy newspapers) that Confederate engineers had rebuilt the Pearl River railroad bridge at Jackson.[9] "If you permit the enemy to regain the use of that bridge and the Mississippi Central Railroad," he warned, "you need not expect military favors from General Grant or myself."[10] Sherman argued that it would be good policy to send out from Natchez, Vicksburg, or Yazoo City, each week, a flying column to insure that no through trains were running on the north-south railroad passing through Jackson. With Forrest either pinned down in north Mississippi or en route to raid his "Army Group's" supply line, Sherman believed that all Slocum needed to be concerned about were Brig. Gen. W. Wirt Adams's and Col. John L. Logan's cavalry brigades, and Brig. Gen. Samuel J. Gholson's Mississippi State Troops.[11]

8 Ibid., 149.

9 Sherman's troops had destroyed this bridge on May 15, 1863.

10 Slocum's District of Vicksburg was a geographic part of Sherman's Military Division of the Mississippi.

11 Unknown to Sherman, Col. John S. Scott had replaced Logan as commander of Confederate forces in the District of Southwest Mississippi and East Louisiana.

Vicksburg, Sherman chided, unless it was used as a base for raids into Mississippi, was of no use whatever to Union forces. Moreover, he considered "the railroad bridge at Jackson" of more value to "the Confederacy than all the population of Vicksburg." Unless all the Negro troops had disappeared, Slocum had sufficient manpower to send out weekly expeditions. "Every soldier," he scolded, "should be doing something against the enemy this summer to keep him busy and from re-enforcing Lee and Johnston."[12]

Maj. Gen. James B. McPherson, who led one of the armies under Sherman, cautioned Slocum that the Rebels would reoccupy Jackson in force, because of the psychological effect it would have on Mississippians rather than for strategic reasons.[13] Should Jackson become the headquarters for a major Confederate military department and if newspapers were again published there championing opposition to the United States government, the city was to be "visited in force."[14]

General Canby advised Slocum that he would move against Mobile on July 6; that A. J. Smith planned to leave La Grange about the 2d; and that a powerful mounted column was being readied at Morganza, Louisiana, to sweep through the Piney Woods and cut the Mobile & Ohio around Buckatunna. Slocum was to cooperate by employing all the horsesoldiers he could spare for a demonstration toward Jackson.[15]

12 Ibid., 150-151. In Virginia, General Grant with three armies was hammering away at Gen. Robert E. Lee's Army of Northern Virginia, while Sherman's "Army Group" was operating against Gen. Joseph E. Johnston's Army of Tennessee on the approaches to Atlanta.

13 McPherson also commanded the Department of the Tennessee, a territorial command to which the District of Vicksburg was assigned.

14 Ibid., 151.

15 Ibid., 151-152.

Canby's plans, however, had to be scrapped on July 1. On that date he received a message from Chief of Staff Henry W. Halleck in Washington, dated June 24, directing him to rush 20,000 troops to the Virginia theatre of war. As the attack on Mobile was to be a joint army-navy undertaking, Canby notified Rear Admiral David G. Farragut that the operations against Mobile had been suspended. The chief quartermaster was told to charter sufficient vessels to embark the First and Second Divisions of the XIX Corps, while Col. Edmund J. Davis, who was to lead the mounted column against the Mobile & Ohio, was notified of the change in plans.[16]

Sherman's and McPherson's messages of June 28 reached Vicksburg on July 2, several days before a courier arrived with news that Canby had been compelled to call off, for the time being, the attack on Mobile. Slocum was understandably miffed by the tone of Sherman's communication. Replying, he pointed out that upon assuming command at Vicksburg, he had sent Brig. Gen. John McArthur up the Yazoo Corridor with a strong column to break the Mississippi Central Railroad. A report describing this operation had been forwarded to General McPherson.[17]

While McArthur was absent from the city, General Canby had stopped off in Vicksburg and had shown Slocum his orders placing him in charge of the newly constituted Military Division of West Mississippi. As Canby interpreted his orders as placing the District of Vicksburg within the limits of his command, Slocum had looked to him for instructions rather than Sherman. Canby's call for 2,000 soldiers had made it impossible for Slocum to send a column to Jackson or against the Mississippi Central.

16 *O.R.*, Series I, Vol. 41, pt. 2, 3, 4, 5.

17 For a detailed account of McArthur's expedition, see Edwin C. Bearss, "McArthur's Expedition Against the Mississippi Central Railroad," *The Journal of Mississippi History*, Vol. 28, No. 1, 1-14.

But on receipt of Sherman's June 28 communication, Slocum had alerted his ranking subordinate, Brig. Gen. Elias Dennis, to organize and outfit a force of 3,500 effectives. With these troops, Slocum planned to cross the Big Black on July 3 and advance on Jackson. A staff officer would leave immediately to explain to Canby that it was now impossible to send him the 2,000 soldiers called for on June 16.

Taking cognizance of the hot-tempered Sherman's statement about "military favors," Slocum explained that he would "continue faithful in the discharge of my duty, which, I think, you readily perceive a very disagreeable and difficult one when you compare the different orders issued to me by General Canby with those issued by yourself."[18]

General Dennis in the meantime had organized a three-brigade division, numbering 2,200 infantry, 600 horsesoldiers, and one six-gun battery—Company L, 2d Illinois Light Artillery. On the 2d, as soon as the troops had drawn their rations and ammunition, Dennis marched his division eastward, via the Jackson road. Nightfall found the bluecoats camped on the high ground overlooking the Big Black. During the day, the pioneers had thrown a pontoon bridge across the river.

The next morning, the column crossed the Big Black and marched eastward. Recruits on their first expedition saw the charred piles of the old railroad bridge and the gutted and fire-blackened hulks of *Paul Jones*, *Charm*, and *Dot*, destroyed in May 1863 at the battle of the Big Black. It was a hot, humid day and the soldiers, in their heavy wool uniforms, suffered from the heat and dust. Tramping through Edwards Station and crossing Bakers Creek, the Federals passed over Champion Hill. Veterans of that hard-fought struggle had difficulty locating points of

18 *O.R.*, Series I, Vol. 39, pt. 2, 160-161.

interest, because of the rapidity with which the vegetation reclaimed the area.

General Slocum and his staff now overtook the column. They had left Vicksburg that morning, but at that hour they were still ignorant of Canby's change in plans. General Dennis reported to Slocum that so far only a few Confederate horsemen had been sighted by his scouts. The Rebels kept their distance, but he was certain that news of the Union march had reached Jackson. The Federals halted for the night on Bakers Creek, a short distance southeast of Bolton.[19]

The advance was resumed on the 4th. One year ago Vicksburg had surrendered and several of the units with the column had led the march into that fallen Rebel stronghold. Four miles west of Clinton, Slocum's vanguard was fired on by Confederate sharpshooters. The Federals pressed ahead, and the butternuts remounted and fell back. At frequent intervals throughout the remainder of the day, the cavalry screening the column was in contact with Rebel horsemen. Shots were exchanged at extreme ranges, and the Southerners would pull back as soon as the Federals started to deploy. It was clear to Slocum and his officers that the foe was endeavoring to slow the march to allow their generals to concentrate a force for the defense of Jackson. After pushing into Clinton, Slocum called a halt and his troops camped on the hills east of town.[20]

19 Ibid., 683; *O.R.*, Series I, Vol. 39, pt. 1, 242-243, 244; Vicksburg *Daily Herald*, July 12, 1864; R. L. Howard, *History of the 124th Regiment Illinois Infantry Volunteers, Otherwise Known as the "Hundred and Two Dozen," from August 1862, to August 1865* (Springfield, 1880), 232-233; Edwin M. Main, *The Story of the Marches, Battles and Incidents of the Third United States Colored Cavalry* . . . (Louisville, 1908), 175.

20 *O.R.*, Series I, Vol. 39, pt. 1, 242-243, 244; Vicksburg *Daily Herald*, July 12, 1864; Main, *The 3d U.S. Colored Cavalry*, 175. Maj. Horace P. Mumford of the 5th Illinois Cavalry led Slocum's cavalry brigade, which consisted of detachments from the 5th and 11th Illinois, 2d Wisconsin, and 3d U.S. Colored Cavalry Regiments.

BRIG. GEN. WILLIAM WIRT ADAMS

The former banker and politician commanded the brigade tasked with defending southern Mississippi.

Library of Congress

Slocum's apprehension regarding Confederate plans to concentrate against his column was sound. On June 22 Maj. Gen. Stephen D. Lee, the Confederate officer charged with responsibility for operations in the Department of Alabama, Mississippi, and East Louisiana, had contacted his ranking subordinate in western Mississippi, Brig. Gen. W. Wirt Adams. Adams was to move all of Brig. Gen. Samuel Gholson's brigade of Mississippi State Troops, except about 500 men, to West. There Gholson would hold his brigade ready to rush to General Forrest's support in northeast Mississippi. The 500 mounted men to be left behind were to watch the crossings of the Big Black and delay any Union column coming out of Vicksburg toward Jackson or Yazoo City. One-half of Col. John S. Scott's effective force was to be called up from Clinton, Louisiana, and concentrated in and around Brookhaven. Adams, himself, was to remain for the time being in Jackson, but he was to hold himself ready to take the field in north Mississippi should it become necessary.[21]

21 *O.R.*, Series I, Vol. 39, pt. 2, 659-660. General Lee on June 23 was promoted from major general to lieutenant general and formally assigned to command the Department of Alabama, Mississippi, and East Louisiana. Ibid., 660.

In the period June 22-July 2, Wirt Adams concentrated the remainder of Scott's brigade at Brookhaven.[22] With cars operating over the tracks of the New Orleans, Jackson, and Great Northern Railroad, it would be possible to rush Scott's brigade to Jackson should the Federals cross the Big Black. Gholson's brigade, except the 500 men patrolling the countryside between Jackson and Vicksburg, was at West, prepared to move to north Mississippi or return to Jackson, as the situation dictated. Col. Robert C. Wood's small brigade was watching the area south of the Big Black and the approaches to Natchez.[23]

On July 3 Gholson's scouts sighted and reported Slocum's column had crossed Big Black. Adams moved promptly to concentrate against the Federals. Telegrams were sent to Gholson at West and Scott at Brookhaven, telling them to rush their brigades to Jackson. The dismounted men and artillery were to come by rail. For the time being, Wood's brigade would remain where it was, as its attention was directed toward a column of bluecoats pushing out from the Natchez perimeter, via the Hamburg road. Thus the suspension of Davis's raid from Morganza against the Mobile & Ohio had permitted General Adams to concentrate a superior force to oppose Slocum's thrust on Jackson.[24]

By July 5 Scott had reported to Adams, while Gholson's brigade was expected to join before the day was over. Scott's troopers took position on the ridge overlooking and commanding the bridge carrying the Vicksburg road over

22 Scott's brigade consisted of the 1st Louisiana Cavalry, 9th Louisiana Cavalry Battalion, Powers's Cavalry Regiment, 16th Louisiana Mounted Infantry, Ogden's Louisiana Cavalry Battalion, and Lay's Mississippi Cavalry Regiment. Howell Carter, *A Cavalryman's Reminiscences of the Civil War* (New Orleans, 1900), 107.

23 Wood's brigade included Wood's Mississippi Cavalry Regiment and Moorman's Mississippi Cavalry Battalion.

24 *O.R.*, Series I, Vol. 39, pt. 2, 683.

Lynch Creek, three miles west of Jackson. Three guns (two 6-pounders and one 12-pounder howitzer) manned by Company A, 1st Mississippi Light Artillery, were unlimbered on Wright's farm.[25]

General Slocum on July 5 resumed the advance. The cavalry was turned into a road north of the railroad, while the infantry division, spearheaded by the 124th Illinois, marched via the Jackson road. The two roads, which were parallel, converged five miles west of Jackson. At the junction, the 2d Wisconsin Cavalry, which had the lead, encountered a roadblock manned by Gholson's people. A brisk fire-fight ensued in which the Rebels more than held their own, until the infantry came up. Slocum now sent his entire column, led by the 11th Illinois Cavalry, down the Jackson road. Confederate resistance soon stiffened to the point where the 11th Illinois called for help, and Maj. Jeremiah Cook brought the 3d U.S. Colored Cavalry up at a trot to their support. Passing through the line of the 11th Illinois Cavalry, the blacks advanced rapidly. They soon met and repulsed a charge by 200 Confederates. Counterattacking, Cook's people drove the butternuts back on Adams's main line of resistance. Major Cook was only apprised of the proximity of the foe when the cannoneers of Company A, 1st Mississippi, shelled his regiment at a range of 400 yards. To escape, the blacks were compelled to take cover in the dry bed of Lynch Creek, where they dismounted.[26]

It was about 11 o'clock when the Union infantry topped the ridge overlooking Lynch Creek from the west. While the 124th Illinois was deploying to the left and right of the Jackson-Vicksburg road, the regiment was shelled by Company A, 1st Mississippi Light Artillery. Slocum now rode up, and, after studying the Confederate position,

25 At the battle of Jackson, fought on May 14, 1863, Lt. Col. Peyton H. Colquitt had deployed his brigade at Wright's farm.

26 Main, *The 3d U.S. Colored Cavalry*, 175-176.

determined that it could be outflanked. While the 124th Illinois and the cavalry kept the Rebels' attention rivetted on the Lynch Creek bridge, Col. James H. Coates would take two regiments—the 11th and 46th Illinois—and Battery L, 2d Illinois Light Artillery, and outflank the foe.

Screened by the ridge, Coates's column marched toward the northeast. As soon as he was certain that his brigade had passed beyond the ground commanded by Confederate artillery, Coates wheeled it to the right and crossed the ridge. The 46th Illinois was ordered to the front, and "moved rapidly forward, in advance of every other regiment, across an open field," and to the left of Battery L, 2d Illinois Light Artillery. As it came into line of battle, the regiment was hammered by the Mississippi cannoneers. But on they pushed, until the timber was reached beyond where Wirt Adams had posted two of Scott's regiments—Powers's and the 1st Louisiana Cavalry. A brief halt was made to permit the bluecoats to dress their ranks, before Colonel Coates sent his brigade to the attack.

The Federal battle line swept forward, crossed a belt of timber, forded Town Creek, and entered a field beyond. Here another halt was made to permit the pioneers to cut a road through the timber over which Battery L advanced its cannon. The guns were unlimbered on a ridge, and the redlegs shelled the foe who had re-formed on a ridge north of Jackson covering the Canton road. After about 20 minutes, the butternuts were seen to give ground. Coates called for another advance, and the Union infantry, supported by the battery, started forward. The 46th Illinois outdistanced the 11th Illinois. Even so, by the time it reached the ridge formerly occupied by the foe, Scott's brigade had retreated up the Canton road.

General Slocum now called for his brigade commanders to re-form their units and the march into Jackson was resumed. The troops suffered greatly from the heat, as they tramped forward and occupied the city.[27] They went into camp near Pearl River, and "fared well" in the city's "luxuriant shades after their exhausting march." Slocum kept a tighter rein on his troops than Generals Grant and Sherman had during the three previous occupations of Jackson: no houses were burned, there was no violence, and the Yanks "took only soldiers' spoils—poultry, fruit, and vegetables." One man recalled:

> The citizens of Jackson seemed very fearful lest they should somewhere upon their premises encounter the terrible Negro in blue. Yet that personage darkened no forbidden doors, and everywhere was as unthreatened and peaceful as a cloudless sky. No one in fact was inclined to add anything to the distress of that beauty in reduced circumstances, the Capitol of Mississippi. The elegant suburban residences are gone, and their ashes are monumented by crumbling chimneys. The business squares of the city are heaps of rubbish. The streets are deserted save by women, by men too old and boys too young for the army, and by the fangless, envenomed wretches who were too turbulent-souled for peace, too mean-spirited for war.[28]

Slocum early on July 6 organized his command into fatigue details. The one from the 124th Illinois was instructed to destroy the railroad bridge across Pearl River. While the soldiers were dismantling the structure, they came under fire from Rebel sharpshooters posted in the underbrush on the east bank of the river. Although a number of men were killed or wounded, the regiment by noon had completed its task.[29] Slocum, who had examined the bridge, was of the opinion that it "was designed merely for temporary use, probably

27 *O.R.*, Series I, Vol. 39, pt. 1, 244; Vicksburg *Daily Herald*, July 12, 1864; Howard, *History of the 124th Illinois*, 233; Main, *The 3d U.S. Colored Cavalry*, 126.

28 Vicksburg *Daily Herald*, July 12, 1864.

29 Howard, *History of the 124th Illinois*, 233.

for the purpose of transferring the rolling-stock from the Mississippi Central Railroad to their eastern roads."[30]

Slocum, having completed his mission in the Jackson area, started his column back to Vicksburg at 4 p.m. on the 6th. The division marched out Capitol Street with bands playing and banners snapping in the breeze. As the rearguard was passing the Deaf & Dumb Asylum, west of the depot, a citizen climbed to the top of the Capitol's cupola and waved a white handkerchief as a signal to Wirt Adams's cavalry massed on the hills north of the city. He was shot from his perch by a member of the provost guard, who had lingered to round up stragglers.[31]

The Union officers expected trouble on the return march. Slocum, Dennis, and the other leaders had learned from the citizens that Adams had rallied "a considerable force consisting of Scott's, Gholson's, and Wood's brigades, supported by Company A, 1st Mississippi Light Artillery," to harass the column "and at the very least to borrow considerable transportation and stores from Uncle Sam." Slocum, knowing that the Confederates were concentrating to the north, determined to camp for the night three miles west of Jackson, near the Lynch Creek bridge.[32]

Major Mumford's cavalry brigade, spearheaded by the 3d U.S. Colored Cavalry, had the advance. The horsesoldiers were followed closely by Col. Benjamin Dornblaser's brigade. While the Federals had been in Jackson, Wirt Adams had rallied Scott's brigade near Canton, where he was reinforced by Gholson's brigade of Mississippi State Troops brought down from West. Adams then moved his command into position near Lynch Creek and prepared to intercept the Yankees. Alerted by his scouts, Adams established a

30 *O.R.*, Series I, Vol. 39, pt. 1, 243.

31 Vicksburg *Daily Herald*, July 12, 1864.

32 Ibid.

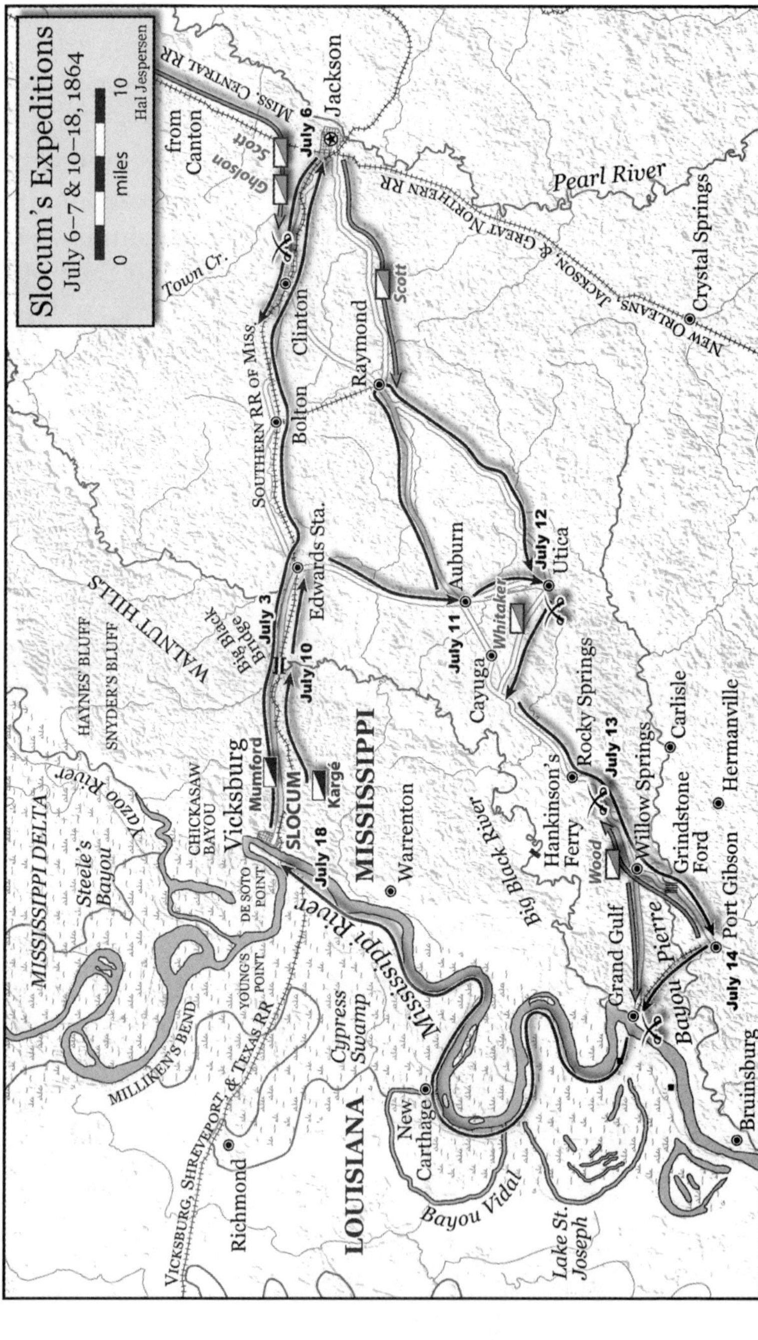

Slocum's Expeditions
July 6–7 & 10–18, 1864
0 miles 10
Hal Jespersen
Miss. Central RR
from Canton
Jackson
July 6
Scott
Gholson
Town Cr.
Clinton
Bolton
Raymond
Southern RR of Miss.
Pearl River
New Orleans, Jackson, & Great Northern RR
Crystal Springs
Edwards Sta.
July 3
Big Black Bridge
July 10
Auburn
July 11
July 12
Utica
Whitaker
Cayuga
Walnut Hills
Haynes' Bluff
Snyder's Bluff
Rocky Springs
July 13
Carlisle
Hermanville
Willow Springs
Grindstone Ford
Hankinson's Ferry
Wood
Big Black River
Port Gibson
July 14
Grand Gulf
Bayou Pierre
Bruinsburg
Vicksburg
Mumford
Slocum
Kargé
July 18
Mississippi
Warrenton
Mississippi Delta
Yazoo River
Chickasaw Bayou
Steele's Bayou
De Soto Point
Young's Point
Mississippi River
Milliken's Bend
Vicksburg, Shreveport, & Texas RR
Cypress Swamp
Richmond
Louisiana
New Carthage
Bayou Vidal
Lake St. Joseph

Major General Henry Slocum's expeditions, mounted from Vicksburg, were designed to divert Rebel attention away from other Federal movements, especially A. J. Smith's push to Tupelo. Slocum broke up the Mississippi Central Railroad at Jackson and diverted Confederate troops from moving to join Forrest.

---

roadblock—Lt. Frank Johnston's cannoneers of Company A, 1st Mississippi Light Artillery, emplaced their 6-pounder guns at the steam-mill, while Lt. Philip B. Lancaster's unlimbered their 3-inch rifles in front of Lee's house.

The Confederate artillerists, who had masked their guns, held their fire until the Union infantry was in view. Their first shot came near unhorsing Lt. Col. J. H. Howe of the 124th Illinois. While the soldiers of the 124th Illinois were taking cover in the woods, Rebel horsesoldiers of Col. John McGuirk's regiment made a slashing attack on the Union cavalry. The 3d U.S. Colored Cavalry was forced back. Mumford committed the rest of his horsesoldiers, but they were unable to check the foe, and the Union cavalry was driven back on Dornblaser's infantry.

To stabilize the situation, Dornblaser sent the 46th and 76th Illinois forward at a quick-step. Skirmishers were deployed and thrown out as the two regiments formed into line of battle and advanced about one-half mile. A halt was then called, while Union skirmishers and the Rebels banged away, burning a great quantity of powder but inflicting few casualties. When darkness closed in, Slocum, after seeing that his brigade commanders had established and manned a strong picket line, recalled Dornblaser's brigade, and the troops were permitted to bivouac in Barrett's field, resting on their arms.[33]

33 *O.R.*, Series I, Vol. 39, pt. 1, 243, 244; Howard, *History of the 124th Illinois*, 233; Vicksburg *Daily Herald*, July 12 and 23, 1864; *Mississippi Statistical Register* (Nashville, 1908), 847, 860, 903; Main, *The 3d U.S. Colored Cavalry*, 176-177. It had taken Gholson's brigade three days to make the march from

An early reveille was held in the camps on July 7. General Dennis by 4 a.m. had formed his division, and when Slocum gave the word, the march was resumed. As the vanguard approached the junction with the Canton road, the Federals again encountered Adams's division. The guns of Battery L were brought into action, as Dornblaser deployed his brigade to the left of the road. The cannoneers of Johnston's and Lancaster's sections hammered back at the Federals with shot and shell. Lt. Col. John J. Jones of the 46th Illinois reported, "For about three hours the regiment remained under this galling fire, showing no disposition on the part of officers or men to swerve a hair, while numbers of the men on the skirmish line and in the line of battle were killed and wounded."[34]

Capt. Henry L. Field of the 124th Illinois had taken cover in the woods. He vividly recalled the bombardment:

> A few colored gentlemen, cooks, or officers' servants were with our forces, who were by no means fond of flying cannon shot. One of these darkies was large, awkward, and wore an enormous white linen duster. He was anxious to get through the woods, or at least to some portion farther west, and was watching his chances between shots, seeming to conclude, as well he might, that the rebels were making his great white coat a special mark for target practice, and that the day of final reckoning with him was close at hand. As this interesting gentleman was jumping from tree to tree, trying to dodge the big balls, and had just taken refuge behind an unusually large one, looking out first to one side, and then the other, with a terribly puzzled and distressed looking countenance, a cannon shot, with a horrid noise, came tearing through the limbs and bushes, when the darky sprang out to one side, then, expecting to be hit if he

---

West. In addition, it had been 36 hours since the troopers and their mounts had had anything to eat. Adams, in the fight, posted his men along the crest of a ridge, where their movements were partially screened by a hedge-row.

34 *O.R.*, Series I, Vol. 39. pt. 1, 243, 244-245.

> went that way, back to the other, and when about half way between two large trees, the ball cutting off a large limb over his head, in an instant, as for dear life, he fell flat on his belly, with arms and legs widely spread out, and white coat covering about a square rod on the ground. But as soon as he decided that he was not killed, he sprang to his astonished feet, and disappeared in far less time than it takes to tell it.[35]

The wagon-master took advantage of the holding action fought by Dornblaser's brigade and Battery L to proceed westward toward Clinton. The road had been reopened by a charge of the 8th Illinois, which compelled the gunners of Company A, 1st Mississippi Artillery, to limber up their pieces and withdraw out of range. After the last wagon had passed the junction of the Canton and Vicksburg roads, Colonel Dornblaser recalled his brigade, and the regimental commanders re-formed their units on the road. The brigade would cover the column's rear as it marched toward Clinton.

After the Federal rearguard had passed through a belt of timber, Wirt Adams advanced Gholson's Mississippi State Troops in an effort to stampede the bluecoats and capture the train. Two of Gholson's regiments pressed forward north of the Vicksburg road and two to the south. The hard-driving Rebels pressed the pursuit so hard that Dornblaser had to halt and deploy his brigade into battle line. The brigade continued the retreat for about one mile, with its back to the train and its face to the foe, Gholson now called for a charge. The 11th Illinois Infantry at this time, supported by two guns of Battery L, was nearest the foe, with the 46th Illinois 300 yards farther west. Spearheaded by Col. W. W. Lowry's 2d Regiment Mississippi State Cavalry, Gholson's people rode down on the Yankees at a gallop. Colonel Jones of the 46th Illinois about-faced his regiment and double-timed to the assistance of the 11th Illinois. Unlimbering two

35 Howard, *History of the 124th Illinois*, 234-235.

guns, the redlegs of Battery L ripped Lowry's regiment with double charges of canister. Several crashing volleys delivered by the two Illinois regiments at a range of 60 yards sent Lowry's people racing to the rear. Two Confederate captains were killed and one mortally wounded. General Gholson received two flesh wounds in the shoulder as he rode up to order a retreat. With Gholson out of action, Col. John McGuirk, as senior officer, took command of the brigade.[36]

Wirt Adams was stung by this repulse, and he was unable to rally his men for another attack. The 46th Illinois now relieved the 11th Illinois as rearguard, and the march toward Vicksburg was resumed. A mile beyond Gholson's repulse, the Federals entered Clinton. While the rearguard was fighting for its life a mile east of the village, one of the citizens had endeavored to signal Scott's cavalry, which was "hovering near the town," with his handkerchief. The train at this time was corralled near Clinton with a small guard. Scott's horsesoldiers, following the signal, dashed into town, but found the train-guard waiting for them. Several saddles were emptied, and the Rebels fled. Slocum, on learning of the incident, ordered the house from which the signal had been given burned and the man arrested. This was the only house destroyed by the bluecoats during the expedition.[37]

Colonel Scott's brigade trailed Slocum's column, at a discreet distance, as far as Bakers Creek, where the Federals camped on the night of July 7. The Yanks on the 8th continued their march westward and recrossed the Big Black, where Slocum was hailed by Colonel Karge.[38]

36 *O.R.*, Series I, Vol. 39, pt. 1, 243, 244-245; *Mississippi Register*, 847, 860, 903, 910, 912; Vicksburg *Daily Herald*, July 12, 23, 1864. General Gholson's wounds necessitated the amputation of his right arm. In 1865 General Gholson told members of the 124th Illinois of his chagrin at the Confederates' failure to "gobble us up." Howard, *History of the 124th Illinois*, 234.

37 Vicksburg *Daily Herald*, July 12, 1864.

38 *O.R.*, Series I, Vol. 39, pt. 1, 245; *O.R.*, Series I, Vol. 39, pt. 2, 168.

The tangible result of Slocum's expedition had been the destruction of the railroad bridge the Rebels were rebuilding across Pearl River, but there was an intangible that was much more vital. Gholson's brigade, which was en route to join General Forrest in northeast Mississippi, had to be recalled to participate in the defense of Jackson. Gholson's rugged fighters would have been a valuable increment to the force Generals Lee and Forrest hurled against the Federals at Tupelo on July 14. The wanton destruction of private property that had characterized the three previous occupations of Jackson and caused the city to be referred to as "chimneyville" was missing on this occasion. Slocum kept a tight rein on his troops, and even the Confederates were compelled to admit that while the foe took off almost every Negro in Jackson, he committed no depredations.

The editor of the Brandon Republican summed up Confederate reaction to the raid:

> We think this a disgrace to the State of Mississippi and the Confederate Government that this little squad of Yankees were permitted to penetrate to the capitol of the state and return to Vicksburg almost unmolested.
>
> Several officers have stated the affair on the part of Wirt Adams was "very badly managed." The charge near Clinton was made by 100 men of Lowry's regiment on a Yankee battery, supported by four regiments. They charged through an open field to within 20 steps of the battery, when they were ordered to retreat after having lost 35 killed or wounded.[39]

Union losses in the expedition were: 33 killed, 156 wounded, and 30 missing. The Confederates listed their casualties as between 70 and 80 killed and wounded.[40]

39 Vicksburg *Daily Herald*, July 23, 1864.

40 Ibid.; *O.R.*, Series I, Vol. 39, pt. 1, 243.

7

General Ellet Finds Colonel Wood at Coleman's Plantation

TO ENSURE the success of the thrust on Jackson and keep Col. Robert Wood's Confederate brigade pinned down in Claiborne and Jefferson counties, General Slocum proposed to employ Brig. Gen. Alfred Ellet's Mississippi Marine Brigade. Ellet was to proceed with his brigade downstream to Rodney, where he would make a landing, and, pushing inland, beat up the countryside and seize cotton. Slocum, to increase the size of Ellet's striking force, issued orders for the 48th and 52d U.S. Colored Troops to embark aboard the boats of the Mississippi Marine Brigade, taking ten days' rations, the regimental wagons, and intrenching tools.[1]

The two regiments, along with the marines, were aboard the amphibious transports by late afternoon on July 2, 1864, the same day that Slocum's column started for Jackson. Ellet gave the signal, and the vessels pulled away from the Vicksburg landing and headed down the Mississippi. Reaching Rodney at two the next morning, the troops thronged ashore and occupied the town. Up till this moment, General Ellet had kept his plans and the division's mission

1 *O.R.*, Series I, Vol. 39, pt. 2, 161. | | The Mississippi Marine Brigade was the creation of Brig. Gen. Charles Ellet, Jr., a pre-war civil engineer who conceived and built the Ram Fleet in 1861. Ellet's rams were not part of the navy, but instead reported directly to Secretary of War Edwin Stanton.

BRIG. GEN. ALFRED ELLET

Ellet commanded one of the war's more unusual formations, the U.S. Mississippi Marine Brigade.

Library of Congress

to himself. The mystery deepened, when, instead of forming the command into two brigades, he organized the troops as they moved out into four divisions: (a) the cavalry battalion led by Capt. John R. Crandall; (b) the two black regiments; (c) a train of 30 wagons; and (d) Col. George E. Currie's mounted infantry of the Marine Brigade. All the men, except those on the flagship, were surprised to see the large number of wagons brought along. Colonel Currie and others shook their heads, because the large number of wagons "precluded all idea of fighting on this trip." In case of a battle, there would not be enough men to engage the Rebels and still protect the wagons. It looked like a cotton stealing foray.[2]

With two days' cooked rations in their haversacks and 40 rounds of ammunition in their cartridge-boxes, the column took up the march toward Oakland College. The weather was hot, necessitating frequent halts for rest and water. About a mile east of Rodney, Crandall's cavalry battalion was challenged and fired on. Crandall's horsesoldiers pushed back the Rebels beyond Oakland College, capturing half a dozen, two of whom were members of the signal corps.

2 *Warfare Along the Mississippi: The Letters of Lieutenant Colonel George E. Currie*, Norman E. Clarke, Sr., ed. (Mount Pleasant, Mich., 1961), 114-115; Warren D. Crandall and Isaac D. Newell, *History of the Ram Fleet and the Mississippi Marine Brigade* (St. Louis, 1907), 424.

It was almost two o'clock before Ellet's division reached Coleman's Plantation, 12 miles from Rodney.[3]

The Coleman house stood north of the Rodney road. Nearby the Rodney-Gallatin road crossed the one leading from Port Gibson to Payette. Ellet told his unit commanders to select their camps and permit their men to bivouac. Colonel Currie camped his mounted infantry in a grove about 500 yards east of Coleman's house, alongside the Port Gibson road. Crandall's cavalry bedded down southwest of the house; the colored brigade to the west; while the wagons were parked in an open field south of, and in front of, the residence. General Ellet chose the house as his headquarters, although it was "occupied by the most rabid of Southern women." Pickets were thrown out, and check points established on each of the roads.

About sundown, General Ellet sent for his unit commanders. They were told to hold reveille early on the 4th, and as soon thereafter as possible Colonel Currie was to start for Port Gibson with his regiment; Crandall's battalion would reconnoiter the Gallatin road; and the Negro regiments and the mountain howitzer would be held in reserve at the crossroads. The night was an uneasy one on the picket line. A few shots were exchanged with unseen Confederates hovering in the shadows, while there were rumors that Colonel Wood was massing his brigade at Red Lick Church.[4]

Reveille sounded at half past three, and the Federals began an early celebration of the "Glorious Fourth." After the men had gobbled a hasty breakfast, the units were formed and moved out. Crandall's and Currie's columns marched

3 *Warfare Along the Mississippi*, 115; Crandall & Newell, *History of the Ram Fleet*, 424-425. The companies of the Mississippi Marine Brigade were left aboard Baltic to guard the transports, when the column drove inland.

4 *Warfare Along the Mississippi*, 117; Crandall & Newell, *History of the Ram Fleet*, 425.

in opposite directions. The morning was refreshingly cool. Currie's route up the Port Gibson road passed "through a community formerly wealthy from the indication, but now the plantations were deserted, and weeds and desolation had taken the place of the busy life and cultivation of a Southern plantation."

Currie's men had ridden about three miles, when a courier thundered up, his horse covered with foam, and told the colonel that Ellet wanted him to countermarch and reinforce Crandall, who was hotly engaged with a superior force on the Galla Road. Currie hastened to carry out Ellet's wishes and returned to Coleman's plantation.[5]

Just at sun-up, Crandall's battalion, after a three-mile ride, encountered the Confederates. Opening fire from ambush, the Rebels peppered away. Crandall called for help. In response to this plea, General Ellet rushed the 48th and 52d U.S.C.T. and the howitzer to the assistance of the battalion. Currie, upon reaching Coleman's, found Ellet standing on the roadside, "greatly agitated at the reports the orderlies were constantly bring[ing] him from the battle ground." Calling to Currie, Ellet ordered, "Take your regiment and move on to their assistance and you are to assume command of all the forces in the field. Should you want me in person, send for me and I will join you without delay." Currie, turning the head of his regiment into the Gallatin road, hurried toward the scene of the fighting.[6]

Meanwhile, reinforced by the two black regiments and the howitzer, Crandall's horsesoldiers broke the Rebel roadblock. The Confederates were pushed back about one-half mile, and, after Colonel Wood called up additional men from Red Lick, they were able to blunt the Union surge. Colonel

5 *Warfare Along the Mississippi*, 116.

6 Ibid.

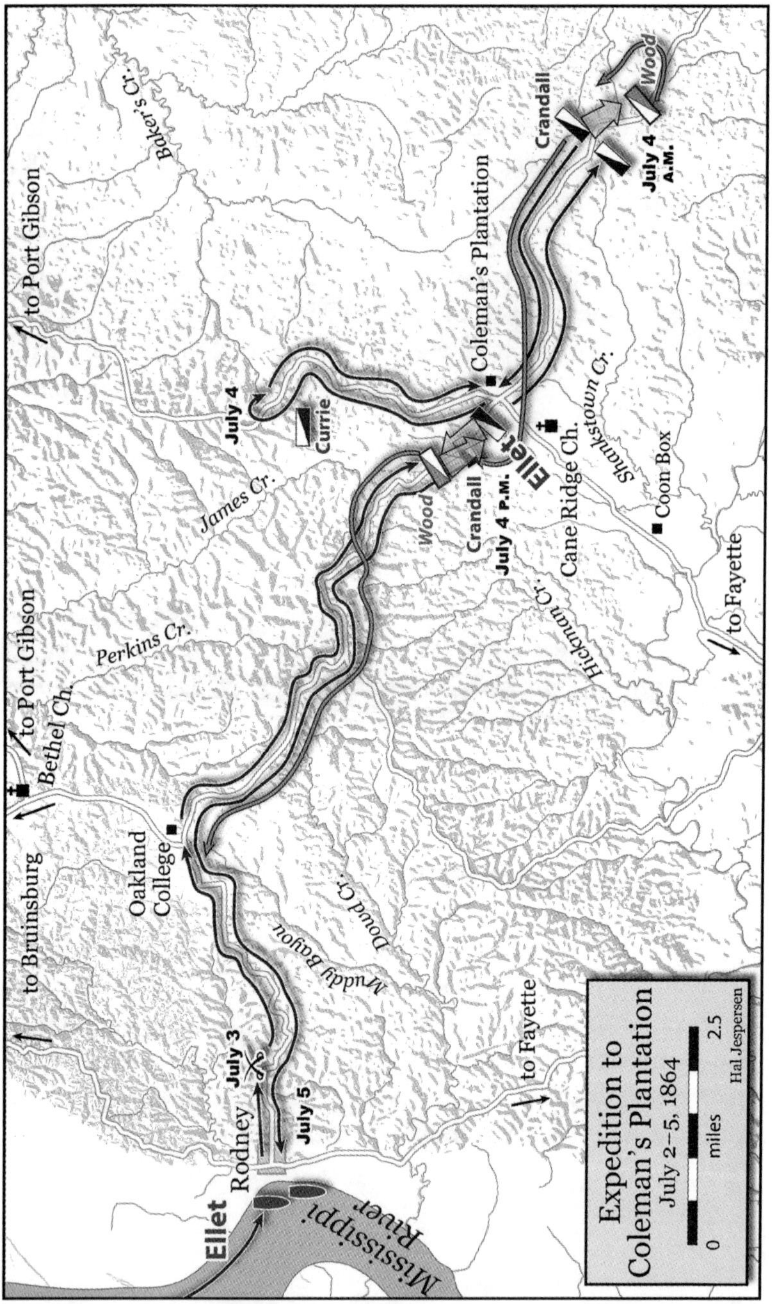

Expedition to Coleman's Plantation
July 2–5, 1864

The Federal Mississippi Marine Brigade's move to Coleman's Plantation south of Vicksburg under Brig. Gen. Alfred Ellet was designed to divert Confederate attention away from General Slocum's own expedition to Jackson. Many Federals, however, believed General Ellet intended to conduct what was little more than a "cotton stealing foray."

Currie and his soldiers, as they pressed ahead saw that the rail fences on both sides of the road had been thrown down

> the result always of a Cavalry fight, and the ground over which they had charged was litterally [sic] plowed up, with here and there and everywhere dead and wounded horses, while a half a mile beyond, both armies apparantly [sic] exhausted were resting in sight of each other.[7]

Colonel Currie made a hurried estimate of the situation. Although Crandall's battalion and the Negroes had gained ground, they had suffered heavier losses. To reach the head of the column, Currie passed along the line of cavalry, now dismounted, and saw that the horses and men were badly jaded and suffering from "the burning rays of a Southern sun." The Negroes were in position to relieve Crandall's people in the event the Confederates renewed the battle.

Col. F. M. Crandal of the 48th U.S.C.T., although he was senior to Colonel Currie, asked him to take charge, as he was more familiar with "this mode of warfare." Crandal then pointed out the Rebels, whose lines were formed on the brow of a hill in a skirt of woods, north of the road. Currie now deployed as skirmishers two companies of U.S.C.T. to the left of the road; the remainder of the blacks were massed in support. The mountain howitzer was positioned on a knoll to the right of the road and sighted to enfilade the Confederates' left; Currie's regiment was posted near the gun, while Crandall's horse-marines were in reserve.

7 Ibid., 116-117; Crandall & Newell, *History of the Ram Fleet*, 425-426.

As soon as all units were in position, Colonel Currie waved his battle line forward. Not a shot was fired until the skirmishers closed in on the crest of the hill, when the Rebels let loose with a volley, which was answered by shell from the howitzer. The greyclads then retired into the woods, and the Negro skirmishers charged. Abandoning their position, Wood's men retreated across a field and took cover in a belt of timber. Currie shouted for the U.S.C.T. to hold their gains, while he led his mounted infantry in a futile chase. Currie, having been outdistanced, retraced his steps and returned to Coleman's plantation. Each unit proceeded to its camp; the horses were unsaddled and fed. While the troops were eating, shots were heard on the picket line.[8]

The Confederates, unobserved, had trailed the Union rearguard as it retired down the Gallatin road. Dismounting and slipping into position on a ridge commanding the camps, they had opened fire. As "Boots and Saddles" was sounded by the buglers of the Mississippi Marine Brigade, one of the Negro regiments, supported by the howitzer, marched to help the pickets. By the time the marines had mounted, the fight on the picket line had "assumed an alarming phase and showed the desperate character and determination of our assailants." General Ellet and his staff, accompanied by Colonel Currie, rode out. The mounted infantry was left in charge of Currie's second in command. Dismounting at the foot of a hill, south of Coleman's house, the officers, dodging from tree to tree, gained the picket line. Currie, a veteran of many engagements, took cognizance of the "scattered firing" of the foe, and concluded that this was a feint to divert General Ellet, while Colonel Wood hurled his main column against another point. Ellet, however, disagreed, and ordered Colonel Crandal to call up the 48th

8 *Warfare Along the Mississippi*, 117-118; Crandall & Newell, *History of the Ram Fleet*, 426.

and 52d U.S.C.T. to bolster the picket line. He and his staff then visited the outpost on the Port Gibson road.[9]

As they passed Currie's regiment, they saw that it was formed and ready to march. A short distance beyond Currie's camp, they were stopped by an elderly Negro, who gasped out the frightening news that "forty thousand mounted rebels were passing around the picket line to get into our rear." Ellet now realized that Currie was correct: the attack on the picket line was a blind to enable Wood and his people "to get in our rear on the Rodney road," and to cut the division off from the lightly guarded vessels of the fleet.

Turning to Ellet, Currie said, "We will fight in our rear in less than half an hour. Let's get ready." The general agreed, and wheeling their horses about, they started for headquarters. Currie now rejoined his regiment, which had remained mounted since the first volley, and led it down the road. A halt was called as soon as the rear of the column was in front of Coleman's house.

Meanwhile, General Ellet had sent Captain Crandall's battalion to make a forced reconnaissance of the Rodney road, which was at best a narrow country lane. A characteristic of roads in the loess region of Mississippi is deep cuts. One-half mile west of Coleman's there was such a cut, and here Crandall's troopers found the Rebels. Caught in a deadly crossfire, the horse-marines recoiled. Many fled, while others, keeping their wits, dismounted and took cover in a cornfield near the cut. Colonel Currie recalled that Crandall's people came back in "terrible confusion," as the "narrow passage was filled with men and horses in an inextricable mass, their very numbers their greatest difficulty rather than their chief assistance."[10]

9 *Warfare Along the Mississippi*, 118.

10 Ibid., 118-119; Crandall & Newell, *History of the Ram Fleet*, 426.

General Ellet sat his horse at the crossroads, "a silent spectator until the shots of the advancing foe drove him back." Seeing that he had blundered, he rode over to the head of Currie's regiment, and exclaimed, "Colonel, in the name of God what shall we do?"

"Do? Let's fight," Currie replied. Pointing to the ridge, where the black brigade was formed, he suggested that Ellet bring it up and post it in the field west of the Rodney road. He would then dismount his regiment and whip the Rebels to his front in five minutes. Currie had little hope of accomplishing this, but he wished "to inspire the General with some confidence and restore his presence of mind."[11]

Currie's psychology worked. Instead of sending an aide, Ellet wheeled his horse about, and galloped off to bring up the two Negro regiments. They were brought up on the double, and filed into line of battle on the south side of a field, their right anchored on the Rodney road. Meanwhile, Confederate leader Colonel Wood had formed his men at the north end of the field, his line stretching across the road so that one half of his men confronted the blacks and the remainder faced Currie's regiment. After dismounting, Currie's people left their horses in a sheltered road cut. Currie moved them up in line behind Coleman's house to a rail fence and outbuildings enclosing a cornfield through which it was believed the foe was advancing. The marines were told to hold this position, and cautioned not to fire "until the rebels were so close upon them, each could select his man and not miss aim."

While his men were filing into position, Colonel Currie looked up into the second story window of the house and saw Coleman's daughter signaling the Rebels with her handkerchief. Calling to several of his men, Currie faced them toward the house, and in her hearing, instructed

11 *Warfare Along the Mississippi*, 119-120.

them that if she reappeared at the window to shoot her down. The lady heeded the warning. Currie, accompanied by several men, now entered the house and took station on the second story porch, where they could overlook the entire field. To protect their position, they barricaded it with furniture and mattresses.[12]

The corn was tall and rank and concealed the Rebels from the Federals' view. Moreover, a number of Crandall's horse-marines, after being routed in the road cut, had sought cover in the cornfield, not knowing they were between the hostile lines, and out of sight of Ellet's other units. When the troops, posted on the high ground at Coleman's opened fire, the marines were compelled to hug the ground to escape the minie balls of friend and foe.

North of the Rodney road, Currie's regiment allowed Wood's people to close to within short range, the men gauging the Rebels' position by the "parting and waving" of the cornstalks, as they crunched through it. A crashing volley delivered at short range, followed by a bayonet charge, cleared the field in front of the unit in less than five minutes. Crandall's horse-marines took advantage of the lull following the repulse to scramble to their feet and slip to the rear.

Colonel Wood now assailed the black brigade south of the road. Several fierce assaults were made on the Negroes, but they held firm. As the firing to their front ebbed, while Wood and his unit commanders rallied their men, one of the black regiments advanced, with the cry, "Fort Pillow! Remember Fort Pillow! No quarter! No quarter." The Confederates now gave way, retiring down the Rodney road.[13]

Ellet met with his brigade commanders to discuss his next move. About this time two marines brought in

12 Ibid., 119-120; Crandall & Newell, *History of the Ram Fleet*, 428.

13 *Warfare Along the Mississippi*, 120-121; Crandall & Newell, *History of the Ram Fleet*, 426-427.

a prisoner who had no uniform, but whose pockets were crammed with cartridges, making it evident that what male citizens there were left in the area had rallied on Wood's brigade. As they were 12 miles from Rodney and further delay would see an increase in the size of Wood's force, Ellet determined to return to the fleet immediately.

The sun was setting, as the brigade commanders, having reformed their units on the road, put them in motion for Rodney. The Mississippi Marine Brigade took the lead; followed by the wagon train, into which the wounded had been loaded; while the black brigade and howitzer brought up the rear. General Ellet, who rode with the rearguard, told Colonel Currie, who commanded the advance, "When the rebels attack you, if you need my assistance, send an orderly for me and I will come to the front."

The road to Rodney led through the loess bluffs, passing through a number of narrow cuts, some as much as 20 feet in depth. To prevent an ambush in one of these cuts, Colonel Currie saw that his brigade was one-half mile in advance of the train, with a strong force of flankers thrown out on either side of the road. The first cut was passed without difficulty, but by the time the column had reached a second cut, darkness had closed in. Wood's Confederates now made a savage attack on Ellet's rearguard. With the help of the howitzer, it was repulsed. Other attacks on the rearguard ensued. At each assault, General Ellet called on Colonel Currie for reinforcements, asking for two or more companies at a time, until the brigade "was reduced to a few men who acted as advance guard and flankers." A check was given the Confederates, when General Ellet ordered a fence thrown down on each side of the road, and Crandall's horse-marines were posted in these gaps. The Negro brigade passed on, and as the Confederates thundered into view, they were caught in a murderous crossfire and retreated in confusion. This was repeated several more times, before the column came down off the escarpment about midnight, and, passing through Rodney, reboarded the transports.[14]

A hurried roll call was made, and upwards of 100 of the blacks failed to answer to their names. By daybreak a number of the missing had straggled in, and General Ellet was able to pare down his losses in the engagement at Coleman's plantation to 21 killed and 33 wounded or missing. Colonel Wood filed no report of his casualties, which the Federals estimated to number at least 150. Colonel Currie, a veteran of Pea Ridge, considered the battle on July 4 as "one of the most desperate I engaged in during the war."[15]

Ellet's command spent July 5 at Rodney. During the day, a flag of truce party was sent out to bury the dead, and to arrange for an exchange of prisoners. This party found Confederate pickets posted within a mile of the river. That evening shots were exchanged on the picket line. On the 6th, Companies C and D of Crandall's battalion rode out on a reconnaissance and returned with news: Wood's brigade had been heavily reinforced by Wirt Adams. There was, of course, no truth to his story. When they came back, the horse-marines drove in a fine herd of beef cattle. After the cattle had been loaded aboard one of the transports, the fleet cast off at 10 p.m. and chugged up the Mississippi.

Early the next morning, July 7, Ellet's division went ashore at Grand Gulf and moved out the Port Gibson road. At Bayou Pierre, the march was momentarily barred by a Confederate force which disputed the crossing. Ellet employed his superior numbers and firepower to scatter the Rebels. Leaving the two Negro regiments to hold the crossing, the Mississippi Marine Brigade made a dash into

14 *Warfare Along the Mississippi*, 121-122; Crandall & Newell, *History of the Ram Fleet*, 427-428.

15 *Warfare Along the Mississippi*, 122; Crandall & Newell, *History of the Ram Fleet*, 427-428.

Port Gibson, driving a small number of the foe through the beautiful little town. Ellet, satisfied that the Confederates were not disposed to fight, recalled the brigade and returned to Grand Gulf. On July 8 the vessels again got underway and returned Ellet's division to Vicksburg, where it went ashore on the 9th.[16]

Ellet's expedition to Rodney and the advance inland to Coleman's plantation was significant in that it kept Wood's brigade engaged in Jefferson and Claiborne counties, while Slocum's column advanced on Jackson. If Wood had been able to join Wirt Adams at Jackson on July 6 and 7, Slocum could have been in serious trouble. The activities of Ellet and Slocum kept General Lee from rushing additional troops to strengthen General Forrest's corps as it girded to meet A. J. Smith's advance. If we are to understand Union strategy for coping with Forrest, we must take into consideration the use made by their generals of their bases at Vicksburg, Natchez, and Baton Rouge to send small mobile columns to keep at least three brigades pinned down in southwestern Mississippi.

The fight at Coleman's plantation on July 4, 1864, was a savage affair. In the engagement, two Negro regiments, the 48th and 52d U.S.C.T., acquitted themselves with honor, as they held their ground in the face of slashing attacks by Wood's veterans.

16 Crandall & Newell, *History of the Ram Fleet*, 428-429. In the fighting at Port Gibson on July 8, the Marine Brigade lost one man mortally wounded, and the Confederates one dead and two prisoners.

8

Slocum Puts the Squeeze on Wirt Adams

COL. JOSEPH Karge, to whom General Washburn had given the mission of raiding the Mobile & Ohio Railroad, embarked his brigade on eight steamers at Memphis on July 4, 1864.[1] Washburn's orders were for Karge to proceed to Vicksburg, where he would procure "such aid as is possible from General Slocum and make a dash for the Mobile and Ohio Railroad, breaking up the Mississippi Central while on the way." The latest reports reaching Washburn's headquarters indicated that the Rebel railroaders had the track repaired and trains running between Panola and Jackson and east from Jackson to McDowell's Bluff, Alabama.[2]

The transports got underway on the 5th, and dropped down the Mississippi to Helena, where they tied up for the night. On the 6th the vessels left Helena at daybreak and stopped at White River landing to take on wood. At 11 p.m., several of the vessels, as they chugged downstream, were fired into by Confederate partisans posted on the

1 The steamers on which Karge embarked his troops were: *J. D. Perry*, *J. C. Snow*, *Silver Wave*, *Madison*, *Sunny South*, *Rose Hambleton*, *Tycoon*, and *Shenanoge* | | No such vessel as Shenanoge is listed in the records. This might be the *Shenango*.

2 *O.R.*, Series I, Vol. 39, pt. 2, 164.

Mississippi shore near Bolivar. One man was wounded before the Federals could return the fire.

Vicksburg was reached at 5:30 p.m., on July 7, and the horsesoldiers disembarked immediately and marched out the Bridgeport road to Clear Creek. The next day, the 8th, the brigade rode on to the Big Black, where Karge encountered Slocum's column as it was returning from the Jackson expedition. When Karge informed Slocum that Washburn had given him the mission of making a "dash for the Mobile and Ohio Railroad," Slocum exclaimed, "that is impossible!" and ordered Karge and his 1,000 cavalry to accompany him back to Vicksburg. While Slocum's troops returned to their camps in and around the "Hill City," Karge's brigade encamped at Four-mile Bridge.[3]

Slocum, on discussing the situation with Karge, learned that A. J. Smith's army had marched from La Grange en route down the Pontotoc Ridge to engage and break-up General Forrest's corps. With Smith's column in the field, he would have to make a second thrust across the Big Black and keep the Confederates he had engaged on July 6 and 7 from joining the force General Lee was concentrating to oppose Smith's advance. On July 9 he issued orders for Brig. Gens. Elias S. Dennis and Isaac F. Shepherd to hold their divisions ready to take the field at 4 a.m. on the 10th. When the men moved out, they were to carry on their person "five days' small rations (no meat) and sixty rounds of ammunition." As hard marches were anticipated, no baggage except one blanket per man and one cup for coffee would be carried. Officers were admonished "to confine themselves to what they can

3 *O.R.*, Series I, Vol. 39, pt. 1, 246. Included in Karge's brigade were: the 7th Indiana Cavalry, the 1st Mississippi Mounted Rifles, the 4th Missouri Cavalry, the 2d New Jersey Cavalry, and the 19th Pennsylvania Cavalry.

COL. JOSEPH KARGE

Karge commanded the 2nd New Jersey Cavalry even though he served in the Prussian Horse Guards. The ardent Polish nationalist emigrated to the United States after the failed 1848 revolution.

Library of Congress

carry."[4] Colonel Karge was to report to Slocum on the Big Black on July 10.[5]

The bluecoats were on the road by the designated hour. There was a torrential rain during the day, which slowed the march to the forward staging area. At Big Black Bridge, Karge reported to Brig. Gen. Alfred W. Ellet on the evening of July 10. Slocum had placed Ellet in charge of the 2,000 horsesoldiers that were to accompany the column. In addition to Karge's unit, Ellet's command included the Mississippi Marine Brigade and Major Mumford's brigade. The 4,000 infantry assigned to the expedition were organized into two divisions, one led by General Dennis and the other by General Shepherd.[6]

A Confederate spy, J. C. Howard, was at Dr. Cook's four miles east of Vicksburg, and he had watched the Federals tramp past. He estimated the force at from 9,000 to 10,000 and had heard soldiers boast that they would be in "Dixie tomorrow." All that he saw and heard satisfied him that General Slocum had called out all available troops in and around Vicksburg, including seven Negro regiments, for the

4 *O.R.*, Series I, Vol. 39, pt. 2, 169-170.

5 *O.R.*, Series I, Vol. 39, pt. 1, 246.

6 Crandall & Newell, *History of the Ram Fleet*, 429-430.

expedition. This information was in General Wirt Adams's hands by nightfall.[7]

Slocum's powerful column crossed the Big Black at daybreak on July 11 and marched by way of Edwards Station to Auburn, a distance of 24 miles. Until he reached Auburn, Slocum was unsure of his next move. Before leaving Vicksburg, he had been inclined to march eastward, then turn his army northward, beat up the region between the Big Black and Yazoo, and then occupy Yazoo City. In fact, he had alerted the navy to have boats standing by to transport supplies to Yazoo City. Now he learned from his scouts that a considerable force of Rebel cavalry, Col. Robert Wood's brigade, was still operating in and around Port Gibson. He determined to move against Wood.

On July 12 the Union column took the field at daybreak and headed for Utica. A patrol from Karge's brigade, screening the army's left, entered Raymond. Confederate scouts were encountered as the bluecoats marched southwestward. There was slight skirmishing throughout the day between these butternuts and Karge's cavalry screening Slocum's infantry.[8]

Soon after the army bivouacked in and around Utica, a Rebel patrol assailed a picket post manned by the Mississippi Marine Brigade. The foe was repulsed with the loss of three killed and four wounded. A house near where the marines were camped was searched, and Confederate uniforms and arms were found. About nightfall three sons of the owner of the house were captured, as they came in to spend the night, being ignorant of the presence of the bluecoats. These men belonged to Capt. Ike Whitaker's Scouts, and much of the time they were in the habit of boarding at home. "This,"

7 *O.R.*, Series I, Vol. 39, pt. 1, 355; *O.R.*, Series I, Vol. 39, pt. 2, 700-701.

8 *O.R.*, Series I, Vol. 39, pt. 1, 246, 256; Thomas S. Cogley, *History of the 7th Indiana Cavalry Volunteers . . .* (LaPorte, 1876), 117; Vicksburg *Daily Herald*, July 23, 1864; Crandall & Newell, *History of the Ram Fleet*, 430.

a Union diarist recorded, "must have been [a] very pleasant way of soldiering."[9]

General Ellet, early on the 13th, sent out several combat patrols to feel for the foe. A battalion of the Mississippi Marine Brigade made a five-mile sweep without seeing any Confederates, but the 1st Mississippi Mounted Rifles of Karge's command was ambushed by a detachment from Wood's Mississippi Cavalry Regiment. The blacks fought their way out of the trap, with the loss of several men, including their commander, Maj. Samuel O. Shorey, who was captured.

Slocum how put his column into motion for Rocky Springs. As on the previous day, Union horsesoldiers screening the advance clashed with patrols from Wood's brigade. Simultaneously, Colonel Scott's brigade, having come down from Jackson, harassed Slocum's rearguard. Nightfall found the Federals encamped on the Port Gibson road, three miles southwest of Rocky Springs. An early start was made on July 14. As the column marched toward Port Gibson, Colonel Wood and his horsesoldiers made no attempt to delay the march. Instead, they harassed the rearguard, Karge's brigade. There was a spirited fight near Rocky Springs that lasted almost an hour. After the bluecoats had gone into camp in and around Port Gibson, one of Wood's combat patrols surprised and captured a 26-man foraging party from the 2d New Jersey Cavalry.[10]

The movements of Slocum's command perplexed the Confederates. At first, General Wirt Adams believed that Jackson was again the Federals' goal, and he concentrated Scott's and McGuirk's brigades for the city's defense. But when the Yankees turned and marched through Utica and on to Port Gibson, he decided that they were out to

9 Crandall & Newell, *History of the Ram Fleet*, 430-431.

10 *O.R.*, Series I, Vol. 39, pt.1, 246-247, 356; Crandall & Newell, *History of the Ram Fleet*, 432; Main, *The 3d U.S. Colored Cavalry*, 181.

"steal cotton," a large quantity of which was stored on the plantations around Utica and Dry Grove.[11]

Slocum on July 15, satisfied that he had kept the Confederate division led by General Adams occupied long enough to ensure A. J. Smith's success against the Confederates in northeast Mississippi, marched his troops to Grand Gulf, where he was to rendezvous with the navy. Two cavalry regiments, the 7th Indiana and the 2d New Jersey, remained in Port Gibson as a rear guard. About 10 a.m. the Rebels attacked the picket line south of town. Col. John P. C. Shanks, after satisfying himself that the last of the infantry had crossed Bayou Pierre, recalled his pickets and evacuated Port Gibson. The citizens signaled this information to Colonel Wood by ringing the church bells. Wood's brigade advanced through the town, cheered on by the inhabitants. Colonel Shanks, employing successive companies to blunt the Rebel onset, fought a skillful delaying action.

General Ellet, hearing the rattle of small-arms, rushed the Mississippi Marine Brigade to Shanks's assistance. At Bayou Pierre, the Confederates, hoping to cut off the escape of the rear companies, came pounding forward at a charge. All the command, except Company F, 7th Indiana Cavalry, had forded the stream. Company F did not panic. The troopers took cover, faced to the rear, and when Wood's brigade swept around a bend in the road, they sent a volley from their seven-shot Spencers crashing into the head of the column at pointblank range. Before the butternuts could recover their wits, the Indianans had escaped across Bayou Pierre.

After the 7th Indiana had forded the stream and had gone into camp, one of Shepherd's Negro regiments established a roadblock on the Grand Gulf road. Before the day was

11 Vicksburg *Daily Herald*, July 23, 1864.

over, the blacks were able to ambush one of Wood's patrols, killing and capturing several butternuts.[12]

On Sunday, July 16, while Slocum's troops were camped at Grand Gulf waiting for the transports, the Confederates mounted an attack on the outpost guarding the Port Gibson road. Three hundred butternuts led by Maj. E. A. Peyton charged the post manned by 30 men of the 5th Illinois Cavalry, supported by a company of the 3d U.S. Colored Cavalry. At the call "to arms," the men of the 3d U.S. Colored Cavalry, the unit camped nearest the outpost, were turned out. Major Cook led his command out on the double and up the steep escarpment. The men were gasping for breath by the time they reached the area, where the men of the outpost were fighting for their lives. One company was rushed to reinforce the outpost, while Major Cook dashed to the left with the remainder of his regiment. Concealed by a ravine to the left of the road, the blacks gained the Rebels' flank. Cook brought his front into line, and the dismounted cavalrymen gave Peyton's people a volley from their carbines, and dashed forward blazing away with their revolvers. The Confederates panicked, took to their heels, and scattered into the brush and gullies. Major Peyton, finding himself deserted by his battalion, surrendered to Lt. Edwin Farley.[13]

Meanwhile, Slocum's infantry and the rest of Ellet's cavalry had fallen out ready for battle. To guard against a renewal of the attack, Slocum posted two of his infantry regiments, the 72d Illinois and the 58th Ohio, in the rifle-pits commanding the approaches to the gutted village.[14]

12 Cogley, *History of the 7th Indiana Cavalry*, 118; Crandall & Newell, *History of the Ram Fleet*, 432. Wood's brigade at this time included: Wood's Regiment, Moorman's Battalion, Stubbs's Battalion, Peyton's Battalion, and a section of Company A, 1st Mississippi Light Artillery.

13 Main, *The 3d U.S. Colored Cavalry*, 180, 182-183.

14 *O.R.*, Series I, Vol. 39, pt. 1, 247, 356; Vicksburg *Daily Herald*, July 21, 1864.

While Major Cook escorted Major Peyton to General Slocum's command post, Major Mumford had the men of the 5th Illinois and 3d U.S. Colored Cavalry take a body count. They reported finding five Rebel dead and eight prisoners, not counting Peyton. When Cook introduced Peyton to Slocum, the general extended his hand and said, "Major Peyton, I am very glad to meet you."

To which greeting, Peyton answered, "I regret very much General that I cannot say the same to you."[15]

By noon a number of transports had arrived, and the infantry and artillery were ordered aboard for the return to Vicksburg, where they disembarked on July 17. Ellet and his cavalry were embarked at noon on the 17th on the vessels of the Mississippi Marine Brigade. The horsesoldiers were put ashore at a point 20 river-miles below Vicksburg, at 5 p.m., and marched up the Warrenton road to within three miles of the city before camping. Karge's brigade on the 18th reoccupied its former camp at Four-mile Bridge, where it remained until July 20, when it rode into Vicksburg and re-embarked on the steamers of the Marine Brigade. The fleet soon got under way. The run up the Mississippi took three and one-half days, and the brigade went ashore at Memphis at 6 a.m. on the 24th, after an absence of 20 days.[16]

Slocum's seven-day expedition from the Big Black to Grand Gulf was significant for it helped contribute to A. J. Smith's victory at Tupelo. But for this expedition, at least one of Wirt Adams's brigades would have been present

15 Main, *The 3d U.S. Colored Cavalry*, 180-181. Subsequently, Major Peyton was exchanged for Major Shorey. Peyton, a resident of Satartia, had served in the Mississippi Rifles in the Mexican War. Among the Confederate dead was a Mr. Wilson, who owned a large nearby plantation and claimed to be a "Union" man, having taken the oath of allegiance. Crandall & Newell, *History of the Ram Fleet*, 433.

16 *O.R.*, Series I, Vol. 39, pt. 1, 247, 356.

in northeast Mississippi during the second week of July 1864. More important, the pressure exerted by Slocum on Adams's district, along with the threat to Mobile, was the decisive factor in causing General Lee to forget his strategy of drawing A. J. Smith's column deeper into Mississippi, and to make his ill-advised assault on the Union position at Harrisburg on July 14.

9

Recommendations

I. Site for Interpreting the Tupelo Campaign

While the present location of the Tupelo National Battlefield Site is not ideal for interpreting the story of the Tupelo Campaign, it is superior to the one suggested in the proposed Master Plan for Natchez Trace Parkway. The ground encompassed in the present site is located about 300 yards to the rear of the position held during the battle on July 14 by Colonel Murray's right flank regiment, the 122d Illinois. It is also close to the position where the gunners of the 2d Iowa Battery unlimbered their guns. The area adjacent to the point where the Parkway overpasses State Highway 6, where it is proposed to interpret the Tupelo Campaign, is not as intimately associated with the fighting on the morning of July 14. The area would be to the rear of the ground from which Crossland's and Bell's brigades advanced to assault Smith's position east of Harrisburg A wayside exhibit here, however, would be more accessible to visitors driving the Parkway than the one at the National Battlefield Site.

We believe there is another site on the Parkway that may be better suited to interpreting the Tupelo Campaign than the present site or the proposed site at the Highway 6 overpass. On July 15 the Federals abandoned their position at Harrisburg and started for Ellistown, via Tupelo. The road

A modern view of the Tupelo National Battlefield Site.

Photo by Bruce T. Klem, Kenosha, WI

followed by the Federals crossed Oldtown Creek, one mile southeast of Clayton's Store. Savage fighting took place here late on July 15. The Parkway passes nearby, and if a site commanding the crossing is available, it would be ideal for interpreting the Tupelo Campaign. Here, the Service would have: (a) ground intimately involved in the fighting; (b) ease of access from the Parkway; and (c) a commanding view.

It is our recommendation that the Tupelo Campaign be interpreted from a site commanding the crossing of Oldtown Creek. Four guns to identify Rice's Battery could be emplaced near the interpretive shelter.

II. Other Interpretive Features

What transpired at Harrisburg on July 14 was dictated by what happened on July 13 on the Pontotoc-Tupelo road and events in southwest Mississippi in the first weeks of July. We therefore recommend (a) that either audio or graphics be used to inform the visitor of the happening

The original panels, which Ed Bearss suggested be replaced, still misinterpret the battle of Tupelo.

Photo by Bruce T. Klem, Kenosha, WI

on July 13, as A. J. Smith stole a march on Forrest; and (b) that consideration be given to erecting a marker near Coleman's plantation. This marker should interpret the story of Union activities in southwest Mississippi that had a vital effect on Confederate strategy and helped precipitate the battle on July 14.

Finally, the current interpretive marker at Tupelo NBS should be redone. For example, undue emphasis is given to Tyler's activities east of Tupelo. People looking at the map and text have been heard to comment that with Tyler east of the Mobile & Ohio the Confederates had Smith all but surrounded on July 14. In reality Tyler's command numbered less than 100 men and constituted no threat to the Federals.

BIBLIOGRAPHY

PRIMARY SOURCES

MANUSCRIPT MATERIAL

Morton, John, Unpublished Memorandum, Morton's Scrapbooks, Tennessee State Library.

Rucker, Edmund, to Morton, John, Feb. 18, 1902, Morton's Scrapbooks, Tennessee State Library.

PUBLISHED SOURCES

Battles and Leaders of the Civil War, edited by Robert U. Johnson and Clarence C. Buell, 4 vols., New York, 1885-1887.

Brown, Andrew, "Historical Sketches," Ripley *Southern Sentinel*, 1934-1935.

Clarke, Norman E., editor, *Warfare Along the Mississippi; The Letters of Lieutenant Colonel George E. Currie*, Mount Pleasant, Michigan, 1961.

Lee, Stephen D., "The Battle of Tupelo," *Publications of the Mississippi Historical Society*, Oxford, 1902.

Mississippi Statistical Register, Nashville, 1908.

Robertson, Melville Cox, "Journal of Melville Cox Robertson," *Indiana Magazine of History*, Vol. 11, 1915.

The War of the Rebellion: A Compilation of the Official Records of the Union and Confederate Armies, 70 vols., in 128 parts, Washington, 1880-1900.

SECONDARY SOURCES

BIOGRAPHIES

Jordon, Thomas, and Pryor, J. P., *The Campaigns of Lieut-Gen. N. B. Forrest*, New Orleans, 1868.

Henry, Robert S., *"First With the Most" Forrest*, Indianapolis, 1944.

Wyeth, John A., Life of Lieutenant-General Nathan Bedford Forrest, New York, 1899.

REMINISCENCES

As They Saw Forrest: Some Recollections and Comments of Contemporaries, edited by Robert S. Henry, Jackson, 1956.

Chalmers, James R., "Forrest and His Campaigns," *Southern Historical Society Papers*, Vol. 7, 1879.

Hubbard, John M., *Notes*, Memphis, 1909.

Witherspoon, William, *Reminiscences of a Scout, Spy and Soldier of Forrest's Cavalry*, Jackson, Tenn., 1910.

STATE AND LOCAL HISTORY

Bearss, Edwin C., "McArthur's Expedition Against the Mississippi Central Railroad," *The Journal of Mississippi History*, Vol. 28, No. 1.

Riley, Franklin L., "Extinct Towns and Villages of Mississippi," *Publications of the Mississippi Historical Society*, Vol. 5.

UNIT HISTORIES

Bryner, Cloyd, *Bugle Echoes, The Story of the Illinois 47th*, Springfield, 1905.

Carter, Howell, *A Cavalryman's Reminiscences of the Civil War*, New Orleans, 1900.

Cogley, Thomas S., *History of the 7th Indiana Cavalry Volunteers . . .*, La Porte, 1876.

Cowden, Robert, *A Brief Sketch of the Organization and Service of the Fifty-Ninth Regiment of United States Colored Troops*, Dayton, 1883.

Crandall, Warren D. and Newell, Isaac D., *History of the Ram Fleet and the Mississippi Marine Brigade*, St. Louis, 1907.

Hancock, R. R., *Hancock's Diary: or, A History of the Second Tennessee Cavalry*, Nashville, 1887.

History of the 9th Regiment Illinois Cavalry Volunteers, edited by Edward A. Davenport, Chicago, 1888.

Howard, R. L., *History of the 124th Regiment Illinois Infantry Volunteers . . .*, Springfield, 1880.

Main, Edwin M., *The Story of the Marches, Battles and Incidents of the Third United States Colored Cavalry . . .*, Louisville, 1908.

Morton, John W., *The Artillery of Nathan Bedford Forrest's Cavalry*, Nashville, 1909.

Reed, David W., *Campaigns and Battles of the 12th Regiment Iowa Veteran Volunteer Infantry . . .*, Evanston, 1903.

Scott, John, *Story of the 32d Iowa Infantry Volunteers*, Nevada, 1896.

Scott, Wm. Forse, *The Story of A Cavalry Regiment: The Career of the Fourth Iowa Veteran Volunteers . . .*, New York, 1893.

Young, J. P., *The Seventh Tennessee Cavalry, Confederate, A History*, Nashville, 1890.

NEWSPAPERS

Brandon Republican

Daily Herald (Vicksburg)

INDEX

About the Author and Editor

EDWIN C. BEARSS was a world-renowned military historian, author, preservationist, and tour guide best known for his work on the Civil War. The grievously wounded World War II Marine served as the Chief Historian for both Vicksburg National Military Park and the National Park Service, authored dozens of books and articles, and led scores of tours each year. Ed helped discover and raise the Union gunboat USS *Cairo* from the Yazoo River, now on display at Vicksburg National Military Park. Ed passed away on September 15, 2020, at the age of 97.

DAVID A. POWELL is a graduate of the Virginia Military Institute (1983) with a BA in history. He has written dozens of books, articles, and historical simulations, including the award-winning *Chickamauga Campaign* trilogy, *The Maps of Chickamauga*, and *Failure in the Saddle*. He is currently finishing the first of what promises to be a five-volume history of the Atlanta Campaign. David and his wife Anne live with their brace of bloodhounds in the northwest suburbs of Chicago.